THE UNIVERSE OF PLATONIC AND PYTHAGOREAN SPECULATION **GARCHES 1234**
WAS COMPOUNDED OF THE SIMPLER RELATIONSHIPS OF
NUMBERS, AND SUCH A COSMOS WAS FORMED WITHIN
THE TRIANGLE MADE BY THE SQUARE AND THE CUBE OF THE NUMBERS 1, 2, 3 . . . .
AND IF SUCH NUMBERS GOVERNED THE WORKS OF GOD, IT WAS CONSIDERED FITTING THAT
THE WORKS OF MAN SHOULD BE SIMILARLY CONSTRUCTED, THAT A BUILDING SHOULD BE
A REPRESENTATIVE, IN MICROCOSM, OF THE PROCESS EXHIBITED AT A LARGER SCALE IN
THE WORKINGS OF THE WORLD. — COLIN ROWE, "THE MATHEMATICS OF THE IDEAL VILLA"

THE CHESS GAME OF ART
THE WHITE KNIGHT OF AESTHETICS
THE BLACK KNIGHT OF SYMBOLICS

HILDNER

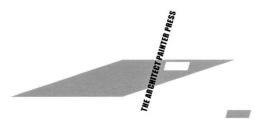

THE ARCHITECT PAINTER PRESS

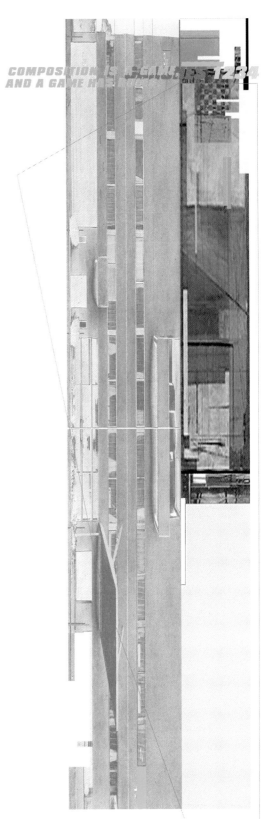

Perhaps the only entirely new and probably the most important aspect of today's language of forms
is the fact that the 'negative' elements
(the remainder, intermediate, and subtractive qualities)
are made active.

— Joseph Albers | CREATIVE EDUCATION[1928]

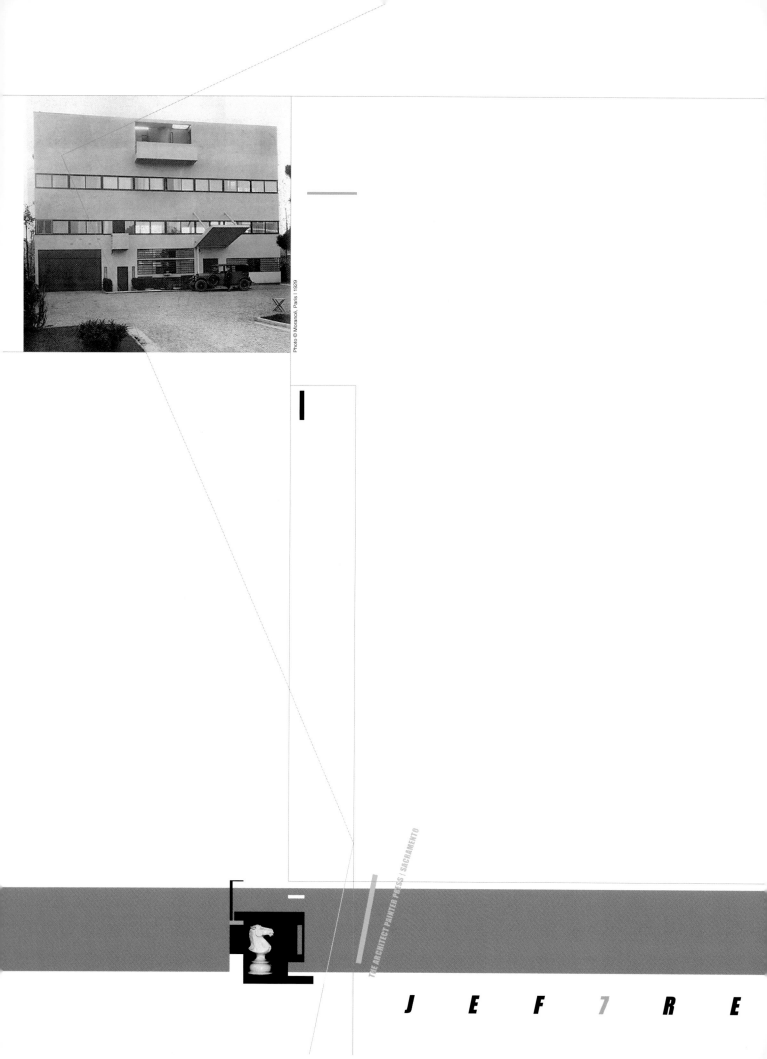

Photo © Morancé, Paris | 1929

THE ARCHITECT PAINTER PRESS | SACRAMENTO

J E F 7 R E

THE ARCHITECT PAINTER PRESS

REMEMBERING THE MATHEMATICS OF THE IDEAL VILLA: AN ESSAY ON LE CORBUSIER'S 1927 VILLA DE MONZIE/STEIN

GARCHES 1234

Y   H   I   L   D   N   E   R

GARCHES 1234 |
Remembering the Mathematics of the Ideal Villa: An Essay on Le Corbusier's 1927 Villa de Monzie/Stein

THE ARCHITECT PAINTER PRESS | **TAPP**
SACRAMENTO, CALIFORNIA
archive.org/details/Jef7reyHildnerArchitect-QFB | thearchitectpainterpress.com | 7@thearchitectpainterpress.com

THIS EDITION CONTAINS MINOR REVISIONS TO THE TEXT, ILLUSTRATIONS, AND LAYOUT.

BOOK CREATED, DESIGNED, AND PRODUCED BY JEF7REY HILDNER
Unless noted otherwise, the author created all photographs, illustrations, and art.

ACKNOWLEDGEMENTS: Thank you colleagues and students whom I acknowledged in earlier versions of this essay— *Association of Collegiate Schools of Architecture Proceedings* (1997) and the *Journal of Architectural Education* (February 1999)—including Colin **Rowe** for his thoughtful comments on an early draft of this study and for his patient encouragement, advice, and insight along the way; Werner **Seligmann** for sharing his personal notes on the site and granting me permission to publish his field-measured site plan; J. Todd Pace, Brad Koerner, and Fred Mason for preliminary help drafting line diagrams; and Emily Beck for early proofreading. Thank you, as well, Denise Bratton and Diane Ghirardo at *JAE* editorial, Janet Hicks at Artists Rights Society, Jennifer Belt at Art Resource, Terri Torretto at Dover Publications, Evelyne Trehin and Michel Richard at Fondation Le Corbusier, and Wim de Wit, Research Library, The Getty Research Institute, for gracious assistance with securing copyright permissions and illustrations; The University of Texas at Arlington (**UTA**) School of Architecture for the opportunity in 1989 to teach a graduate design studio, where the seeds of this book were planted, and for subsequent invitations to explore new ideas in architectural education. Finally, thank you mentor-colleagues George **Gintole** and Richard **Rosa** for inspiring me with your visual intelligence (and thank you RRI11 for helping to verify finer points of the subtle **right shift** that ripples through Garches along its north-south processional axis); Princeton friend and advocate David **Zlowe** for your intellectual and moral support of this project during our work together on *Dante | Telescope House*; Richard **Atchison** of FormFinding Studios for your on-the-same-wave-length aesthetic spirit and collaboration with Cinematect® Studios while I worked on this book; Julio **Rivas** for your metaphysical support along the journey. Patricia E. **Grieve** for your understanding and encouragement during years of research and development; and coinventor of the **0-10 Leonardo Aesthetic Index** (**AKA 0-10 White Knight Aesthetic Index**), my daughter, Emily Madison **Hildner**.

Dedicated to the education of architects — and for all who celebrate what constructivist sculptor Naum Gabo called

E Y E S   E X A C T   L I K E   A   R U L E R

For the original refereed essay on which this book is based, "Remembering the Mathematics of the Ideal Villa," *Journal of Architectural Education*

A R C H I T E C T U R E
is not simply construction, or even the satisfaction of material needs;
it must be something more.
It is the force that disciplines these constructive and utilitarian properties
in order to achieve a much higher aesthetic value.
Architecture will superimpose construction only when the beholder will be forced to stop and observe,
excited and touched by the harmony of proportions in front of him.

— Giuseppe Terragni | 1931

Le Corbusier, Villa de Monzie/Stein, Garches, 1927. Preliminary Studies (L-Scheme), July 1926. **Le Corbusier sketches a special world racing with twin currents—simplicity and multiplicity, precision and play, control and soul; he unspools a skillful matrix of form-space oppositions within the three-dimensional chessboard of the aesthetic field**—inside\outside, building\landscape, ground plane\sky plane, open\(en)closed, public\private, addition\subtraction, horizontal\vertical, front\back, solid\void, planarity\plasticity, site\sight; **he draws a world you can feel as well as see**. © FLC 31480. (See *LCA*, vol. 3, p. 468.)

Architecture is not a business, not a career, but a **_CRUSADE_**
and a **_CONSECRATION TO A JOY THAT JUSTIFIES THE EXISTENCE OF THE EARTH._**

— Ayn Rand | THE FOUNTAINHEAD [1943]

T H E   B A S I S   O F   E V E R Y   A R T   I S   C O N F L I C T

— Sergei Eisenstein | FILM FORM [1949]

L A W S   O F   T H E   M I N D

GREAT BUILDINGS EDIFY. They also strike an emotional chord. They move us. We feel their intelligence . . . and surrender to their deep, poetic power. Complex intellectual-aesthetic systems, inherently visual—an amalgam of the visible and invisible—great buildings speak simultaneously to minds and hearts.

So do great writings. And in the millennia-long literature of architecture, few texts succeed on these two levels— education and emotion—more than those written by one of the twentieth-century's preeminent scholar-essayists, Colin Rowe. His most celebrated essay, though not necessarily his best, "The Mathematics of the Ideal Villa," has been a cornerstone of advanced architectural education since it first appeared in 1947. Rowe's essay functions as the *sine qua non* mental punching bag for my own essay, presented here in its entirety for the first time.

The power of Rowe's essay lies in the dialectical simple\profound structure of its thesis. It unites under one intellectual roof the ostensibly conflicting plastic systems of twentieth-century Paris-based Swiss Modernist architect Le Corbusier and seventeenth-century Italian Renaissance/Mannerist architect Andrea Palladio. Its power also lies in the conceptual and linguistic fiber of its detective-style scholarship. With Raymond Chandler cool (layered over shaggy-dog British erudition), Rowe systematically cracks a case that until he arrived on the scene was not perceived to be a case. And he leaves us blissfully stunned, marveling at the wonder of it all. Add to this his love of the written word and a peculiar and accessible frame of mind that at various turns is simultaneously unequivocal and fuzzy, hesitating and direct, and you have scholarship as edifying page-turner.

Mies van der Rohe said, "God is in the details." The details of Rowe's "Mathematics" essay got my attention 16 years ago. Rowe focused, in part, on one of Le Corbusier's masterpieces, a paradigm of early Modern Architecture, the 1927 Villa de Monzie/Stein in the Paris suburb of Garches (oddly enough, the precise name of the project proves somewhat elusive, if not also controversial—see the end of note 21 of the essay for the backstory—but architects typically refer to the house as Garches, pronounced *Garsh*). Specifically, Rowe focused on the proportional system that Le Corbusier employed for the structural grid of the house. My interest in his analysis began in the fall of 1989 as a result of teaching a graduate design studio at the University of Texas at Arlington. I asked my students to design a supplemental structure and garden for Garches. I called the project "Eliade's Library" because the purpose of the supplemental structure was to house the library of the Romanian historian of religion, Mircea Eliade, whose beautiful book *The Sacred and the Profane* describes the deep, archetypal forces in architecture of metaphor and myth. During my rereading of Rowe's essay and analysis of Garches at that time, I discovered a surprisingly simple new way of looking at Le Corbusier's grid of the house—a way that at once departed from and extended Rowe's view. In November 1989, I made an 18" x 24" drawing that documented this discovery.

The drawing was published in 1990 in *Architecture New Jersey* as part of an article I wrote called "Drawing as Contemplation" (the drawing was also published in *Oz* 12 that same year in a related article, "The Writing of Architecture: Mnemosyne and the Wax Tablet"), and the drawing appears here on page 87. In point of fact, this aspect of the drawing, barely discernible when reduced for publication, was far less important to me at the time than visual expression of the connection between architecture and literature, a connection that operated as an important premise of a subsequent architecture-as-painting project, *Dante/Telescope House* (1991–96)—see photo on page 73— which was published in the spring of 1997 in volume 51 of *Global Architecture Houses*.

Now, in addition to my 1989 discovery relating to the grid of the house, I had begun to suspect that the entire site, which Rowe had not examined, including the disposition of the gate keeper's lodge relative to the main house, was an equally calculated expression of Le Corbusier's mathematical system. Full understanding of this would not dawn on me until many years later. Still, motivated more by intuition than understanding, I charged my Arlington students with the task of rigorously integrating, through consonance and dissonance, their avant-garde form-space inventions into what I perceived to be Le Corbusier's highly disciplined, mathematically controlled, chess-board– like Master-Field—a Synthetic-Cubist buildings-and-landscape matrix. The Cubist aspect, specifically Synthetic

Cubism, by which the entire project (Villa as well as villa) can be viewed as an empty\full (Le Corbusier's words for void\solid) expression of basic ancient-modern principles—*architecture as fragment of a larger whole* and *architecture as space-definer versus space-occupier*—also started to crystallize as I began in earnest in 1991 to write an essay that would explain and perhaps extend my discovery. Over the course of the next seven years I researched, wrote, and endlessly rewrote the essay you see here. I published preliminary versions under the title "Remembering the Mathematics of the Ideal Villa," first in *86th ACSA Annual Meeting Proceedings* (1998) and then in the refereed quarterly *Journal of Architectural Education* (1999)—see the abstract on page 81. *JAE* deleted and misprinted crucial illustrations. So I decided to create a book. **GARCHES 1234** presents my essay in its final, extended, and fully illustrated form.

On my quest, I sought answers that would tie Le Corbusier's entire project together, building and site—a holy-grail **unified field theory**, as it were, that would substantiate my confidence that what Rowe had discovered (and the little Le Corbusier himself had revealed) about Garches's grid was just the tip of the iceberg. Gradually, and not without frustration, encountering dead ends and obstacles here and there along the way, I found it, I believe: the mathematical basis of Le Corbusier's systematic regulation of the horizontal and vertical matrix. I cannot say for sure that I am right. But I am confident that something near to it is right, and some future scholar-explorer, if not I, will eventually nail it down. For we ought not to underestimate the degree to which Le Corbusier meant what he said and said what he meant when he proclaimed that at Garches "proportion ruled absolutely there, as absolute mistress."

I wrote this book mainly for insiders: people cast under the spell of architecture and versed in its theory. My book is by no means comprehensive. Garches presents a subject whose boundaries extend well beyond the frame of this book. But **GARCHES 1234** will, I believe, through its unique twist of the analytical kaleidoscope, reward students, serious scholars, and practitioners of architecture with new insights into subtle, significant dimensions of Garches's mental infrastructure. I also hope that this book will expand professional architects' horizons of self-criticism and inspire recalibration of aspects of one's own form-making strategies vis à vis Le Corbusier's complex intellectual-aesthetic modus operandi.

The highlight of my decade-long stretch working on this project was meeting Colin. I'll never forget the day. It was 1996. We had corresponded about my article for several years. That in its own right had been amazing. Now, on a beautiful, serene spring afternoon in Washington, D.C., we met for lunch at his apartment. I remember little else of our conversation that day other than four words. As I surveyed his rooms of books, commenting on various volumes of interest, and doing much the same in regard to the historical architectural prints and paintings that covered his walls, exclaiming over an especially satisfying fragment here and there, as is my nature, Colin smiled and said, "You're *visual*, aren't you?" In a flash, I understood. That, indeed, was the essence of Colin's special intelligence, what he valued—the visual. Ultimately, it was the phenomenon of the visual and its underlying, sustaining thought-strata that Colin Rowe sought through his scholarship, as a flashlight cuts through darkness, to illuminate. In a modest way, **GARCHES 1234** / *Remembering the Mathematics of the Ideal Villa* seeks to do the same.

When Colin passed on in the fall of 1999, my pseudonymous alter ego Madison Gray wrote the following eulogy. I can't think of a better way to conclude this introduction:

"A WORK OF ART LIVES ACCORDING TO THE LAWS OF THE MIND." —COLIN ROWE

It might be said that Colin Rowe himself, whose essays are works of art, lived according to the same laws of the mind. The visual and the mental provided the double-framework for Colin's special deep view of architecture. How profoundly and uniquely he reminded us and will continue to remind us through his enduring writings of the ennobling truth that "Architecture rests on intellectual as well as material foundations." Has any figure of the twentieth century—or of any century for that matter—contributed more beautifully and substantially to the serious literature of architecture? Are anyone's writings on the art of building more significant, incisive, transforming, inexhaustibly edifying, and reassuring? George Bernard Shaw wrote: "Without art, the crudeness of reality would make the world unbearable." And perhaps no less we may say similarly that without Colin Rowe, without the writings that flowed from his incandescent visual intelligence, the crudeness of reality would indeed make architecture unbearable. Thank you, Colin.

SEE PAGE 81 — TO READ THE ABSTRACT FOR THE ORIGINAL REFEREED ESSAY, "REMEMBERING THE MATHEMATICS OF THE IDEAL VILLA," PUBLISHED IN *JOURNAL OF ARCHITECTURAL EDUCATION*.

THE ESSAY

REMEMBERING THE MATHEMATICS OF THE IDEAL VILLA

HILDNER

Photo © Alfred Roth, Zürich

In a complete and successful work there are hidden masses of implications, a veritable world which reveals itself to those whom it may concern—which means: to those who deserve it.

— Le Corbusier | *A NEW WORLD OF SPACE*

... no serious study of Le Corbusier can be based on the 'official' versions alone. In particular, this is the case for Garches.

— Roger Herz-Fischler | "LE CORBUSIER'S 'REGULATING LINES'"

THE UNIVERSE OF PLATONIC AND PYTHAGOREAN SPECULATION WAS COMPOUNDED OF THE SIMPLER RELATIONSHIPS OF NUMBERS, AND SUCH A COSMOS WAS FORMED WITHIN THE TRIANGLE MADE BY THE SQUARE AND THE CUBE OF THE NUMBERS 1, 2, 3 . . . . AND IF SUCH NUMBERS GOVERNED THE WORKS OF GOD, IT WAS CONSIDERED FITTING THAT THE WORKS OF MAN SHOULD BE SIMILARLY CONSTRUCTED, THAT A BUILDING SHOULD BE A REPRESENTATIVE, IN MICROCOSM, OF THE PROCESS EXHIBITED AT A LARGER SCALE IN THE WORKINGS OF THE WORLD.

— Colin Rowe | "THE MATHEMATICS OF THE IDEAL VILLA"

FIGURE 1 Le Corbusier, Villa de Monzie/Stein, Garches, 1927. Oblique view of the north/street-side facade. © FLC L1(10)45. (See *Oeuvre complète* 1910–1929, p. 141.) The dynamic play of projections defines what I call the **Double-Cantilever Zone**— plastic expression of the crucial yet underappreciated structural-spatial intervals that regulate the primary, north-south axis (the longitudinal site axis) of Le Corbusier's celebrated Villa.

*SEE*s."

— Le Corbusier[1]

THE SO-CALLED ABABA RHYTHM OF THE STRUCTURAL GRID of Le Corbusier's remarkable 1927 Villa de Monzie/Stein at Garches enjoys legendary status in the history of modern architecture. Advanced students of architecture educated in the West over the last fifty years or so are likely to be familiar not only with the Purist-painting–inspired imagery of Le Corbusier's iconic villa. They are also likely to be familiar with the villa's more recondite, yet fundamental, connection to the structural grid of Andrea Palladio's Villa Malcontenta, completed circa 1550–60 during the late Italian Renaissance. Ironically, however, the celebrated essay that brought the connection to light, Colin Rowe's "The Mathematics of the Ideal Villa: Palladio and Le Corbusier compared,"[2] first published in 1947, actually made no reference to the structural intervals in terms of A and B. Commentators on Rowe's essay, not Rowe himself, introduced and popularized the formula ABABA for Garches.[3]

In fact, in keeping with the iconic elevation diagrams published by Le Corbusier in his *Oeuvre complète* (Figure 2),[4] Rowe only used the designations A and B in connection with a related but different mathematical property of the villa—namely, its proportional regulation by the Greek golden section.[5] With respect to the rhythm of the structural intervals running east and west between the villa's end walls, Rowe was equally strict in employing Le Corbusier's own designations, which are indicated on the same elevation diagrams as 2:1:2:1:2. The numerical sequence in contrast to the alphabetical one has the obvious benefit that it not only indicates the rhythmic alternation of bays, but it also relates information about their ratios.

The issue of nomenclature may seem trivial, but it signifies larger issues. It functions as a mental threshold to this essay's central purpose: to heighten perception of the Villa de Monzie/Stein's elegant mathematical structure. One way to frame it is this: With respect to the villa's grid, attention subsequent to Rowe's essay has been focused on the *east-west* structural intervals. Whether designated as ABABA or 2:1:2:1:2, these intervals represent only half the story. But what about the other half—what about the *north-south* structural intervals? A grid comprises intervals running in *both* directions.

Rowe's essay is a cornerstone of architectural education. As a result (factoring in the wide-spread influence of post-Rowe commentators), in architectural circles the association of the villa at Garches with the ABABA or 2:1:2:1:2 rhythm is commonplace. By contrast, knowing the correct answer to the following question is not commonplace: What is the numerical (or alphabetical) sequence of the structural intervals that run in the other direction—the intervals that parallel the principal, north-south axis of the site?

Somewhere along the line, the idea of *the grid as a whole* has slipped through the cracks.[6] It has been forgotten.

Remember that Rowe esteemed the memorable. He spotlights this idea in the first sentence of his essay, describing Palladio's Villa Capra-Rotunda as "mathematical, abstract, four square, without apparent function and totally memorable."[7] In many ways Le Corbusier's house at Garches is also "totally memorable." But this isn't true of its celebrated grid—that is, not as it has been promulgated in the literature of architecture to this point. But I maintain that if it is considered through a new lens, if its mathematical expression is *transformed* or *defamiliarized*,[8] then Garches's grid indeed emerges in razor-sharp focus as a surprisingly easy-to-remember construct. It possesses the quality essential for total recall—*ideality*. Its mathematical structure is pristine. Ultimately, according to my take on the subject, the intervals that define the grid's *abscissae* (the north-south coordinates) are as simple to remember as the intervals that define the grid's *ordinates* (the east-west coordinates).[9] The two systems intercorrelate lucidly, like the bass and treble lines of a Bach fugue. Mathematically interlocked, they constitute an elegant matrix.

In this essay, I propose a new numbering system. My system provides a cogent way of thinking about and remembering the mathematics of the villa that goes well beyond the popular but ultimately misleading ABABA / 2:1:2:1:2 expressions. My system reveals the grid's intrinsic ideality and its nature as an elegant mathematical paradigm, with ancient resonance and corresponding mnemonic power. The new numbering system for the plan of the house provides a springboard for examing other aspects of the villa's proportional substructure. I take a look at the underappreciated end elevations, the site plan, and main facades and show how Le Corbusier interlocked horizontal and vertical fields to form a unified composition that is at once simple and complex.[10]

FIGURE 2 (below) Le Corbusier, Villa de Monzie/Stein, Garches, 1927. Drawings of the north (street-side) and south (garden-side) elevations/facades. © FLC 10453 and FLC 10454. (See *LCA*, vol. 3, p. 394 and *Oeuvre complète 1910–1929*, p. 144.)

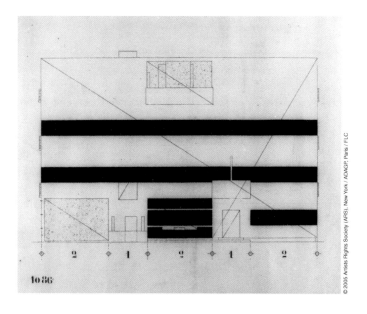

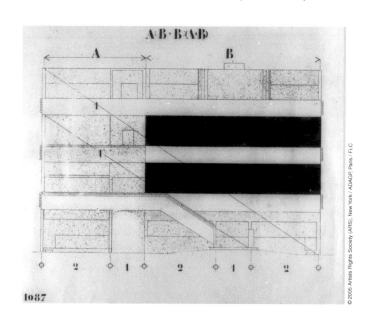

Le Corbusier, Villa de Monzie/Stein, Garches, 1927. Ground floor plan (bottom) and *piano nobile* plan (top). (East is down.) © FLC 10418. (See *LCA*, vol. 3, p. 375.) Note the name on the drawing: **Mme G de Monzie**.

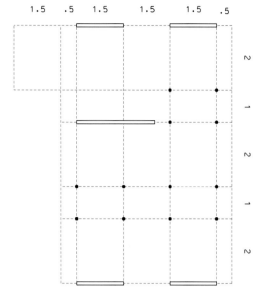

1976

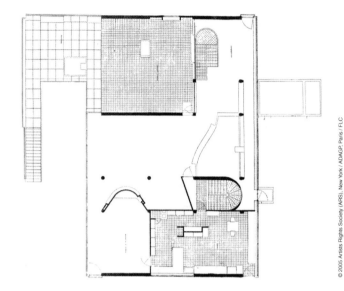

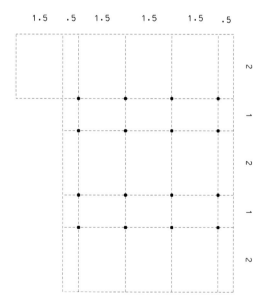

1947

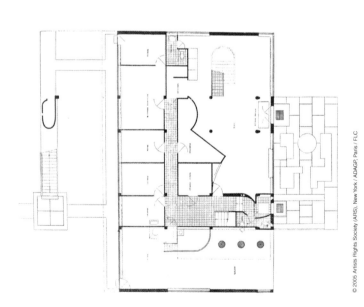

FIGURE 3 (left, top and bottom) Rowe's diagrams (which I have redrawn) of the schematic interval-structure of the Villa de Monzie/Stein's plan, based on Rowe's original illustration for the 1947 article (ground floor) and on the revised illustration published in the 1976 edition (*piano nobile*). In the Le Corbusier-Rowe–based numbering system, the ratios that describe the primary rectangular field of the villa (east-west\north-south) are **2:1:2:1:2** \ ½:1½:1½:1½:½. What I call the **summary sequence** is ½:1:1½:2. (East is down.)

FIGURE 4 (right, top and bottom) Le Corbusier, Villa de Monzie/Stein, Garches, 1927. Ground floor plan (bottom) and *piano nobile* plan (top). (See *Oeuvre complète* 1910–1929, p. 146.) I have added two free-standing columns in the living room of the *piano nobile*; these columns were built but do not appear in the *Oeuvre complète*. (East is down.)

P L A N

CONCEAL | REVEAL

Rowe's famous analytic diagrams of Garches and the Villa Malcontenta, which first appeared in print in 1947, illustrated the schematic interval-structure of Le Corbusier's villa by employing what is ostensibly its ground-floor plan. In the 1976 edition of the article, Rowe illustrated the same schematic interval-structure by employing the villa's *piano nobile* plan. I have recreated both diagrams (Figure 3), which can be compared with Le Corbusier's corresponding plans (Figure 4).[12] One of the significant differences between the east-west intervals and the north-south intervals is that the east-west intervals are contained by the building's primary rectangular field of enclosure. The north-south intervals, by contrast, extend from the building out into the site and thereby function to organize the spatial relationships of various secondary and tertiary phenomena (for example, the projected south terrace that Rowe includes in his diagram, to which he assigns the interval designation 1½).[13] This underscores the all-important organizing function of the north-south axis of the site. With this difference in mind, it is still important to consider the grid in simplest terms as the relationship between the five east-west intervals and the five major north-south intervals, which together describe the building's primary rectangular field of enclosure.

Thus, in the Le Corbusier-Rowe numbering system, the east-west sequence is **2:1:2:1:2**, and the north-south sequence is **½:1½:1½:1½:½**. What I call the *summary sequence*—the numbers in ascending order that represent the four different bay sizes or regulating intervals that Le Corbusier used in the villa—is **½:1:1½:2**. These are the four numbers that are now associated in the literature of architecture with the villa's fundamental numerical structure.

Le Corbusier was clearly attuned to what mathematicians call "elegance," which refers to the aesthetic property of mathematical expressions. So it isn't surprising that he celebrated the 2:1:2:1:2 proportional sequence of the east-west intervals in the *Oeuvre complète*.[14] According to Rudolf Wittkower, the Pythagorean-Platonic tradition regards the 1:2 ratio, which is the ratio of the square to the double square (the point of departure for Le Corbusier's later work on the Modulor), as the basis for all musical consonance: "Perfection and beauty were there ascribed to the ratio itself."[15] Ultimately, Greek ideals of mathematical perfection and beauty value whole-number relationships.

It also isn't surprising, therefore, that Le Corbusier chose to suppress the proportional sequence of the fractional north-south intervals, which are not identified in the *Oeuvre complète*. Nor were the end elevations to which they pertain published (though presumably for reasons that have to do with promoting the north and south facades as the primary architectural events of the vertical field).[16] In fact, one of the most original aspects of Rowe's essay, I maintain, was that he drew attention to the ratios of the north-south intervals, and in so doing, partially revealed what Le Corbusier had concealed—namely, the complete mathematical structure of the grid. But the problem is that the north-south sequence that Rowe revealed—½:1½:1½:1½:½—is awkward and hard to remember. And this is why, I believe, it has been difficult up to now to conceptualize and remember the grid as a whole.[17]

THE CHESS GAME OF ART
THE WHITE KNIGHT OF AESTHETICS
THE BLACK KNIGHT OF SYMBOLICS

MATHEMATICAL SHIFT — 1:2:3:4

Yet, as Rowe may have intended the reader to infer from his diagrams, the inelegant fractions can be eliminated through the simple mathematical device of *doubling*. The following is the result, as my alternative diagrams show (Figure 5). With respect to the five major intervals that describe the grid in each dimension, the east-west sequence is **4:2:4:2:4** and the north-south sequence is **1:3:3:3:1**. The summary sequence is **1:2:3:4**. The device of *doubling* produces a mathematical shift and reveals the intrinsic elegance of the Villa de Monzie/Stein's proportional structure, which is based on whole-number relationships. Clearly, **the grid at Garches is ordered by the first four integers: 1, 2, 3, 4.**[18]

My diagrams differ from Rowe's in other ways as well. They include the suspended entrance canopy (3 + 1) to the north and the extra interval (1) of the terrace to the south, from which the outdoor stairway descends to the garden.[19] These additions heighten awareness of the surprising degree to which Le Corbusier regulated the entire plan through the use of the ratios of the first four integers. According to this numbering system, the primary rectangular volume of the villa oscillates between two readings: (a) At the ground floor, the ratio of the rectangular field is 10:16; (b) At the *piano nobile*, the ratio of the rectangular field is 11:16. Thus, Le Corbusier defines the limits of an extended horizontal rectangular field whose ratio is 19:16.

These alternative diagrams also represent a fine tuning of the villa's structural diagram with respect to the realities of the columnar order.[20] These diagrams reveal the difference between the circumstantial disposition of structure at the "profane" ground floor (thirty-one columns) and the more idealized disposition of columns at the "sacred" *piano nobile* (twenty-two columns). Significantly, neither of these floors nor the two upper floors exhibit the ideal condition of twenty-four columns that Le Corbusier's three-bay by five-bay structural matrix would imply (i.e., four columns by six columns). The five ground floor columns coplanar with the north facade represent an especially significant example of Le Corbusier's circumstantial deployment of columns. Their presence reveals another grid-related surprise, I maintain: The corresponding area of the *piano nobile* above is actually cantilevered only at the northwest corner.[21]

Rudolf Wittkower, on whose scholarship Rowe relied, wrote: **all systems of proportion in Western art and architecture . . . are ultimately derived from Greek thought. Pythagoras, living in the sixth century B.C., is credited with the discovery that the Greek musical scale depends on the division of a string of the lyre in the ratios 1:2 (octave), 2:3 (fifth), 3:4 (fourth) and 1:4 (double octave). In other words, *the ratios of the first four integers 1:2:3:4 express all the consonances of the Greek musical scale*** [my emphasis].[22]

As such, the grid of the villa at Garches, when viewed as based on the ratios of the first four integers, **1:2:3:4**, constitutes an architectural expression of the fundamental relationships of Western musical harmony. Supremely elegant, Le Corbusier's spatial partitioning turns out to be truly in accord with Rowe's description of the Greek ideal, a "universe . . . compounded of the simpler relationships of numbers"[23] —but in ways more iconic and pristine than his diagrams indicate.

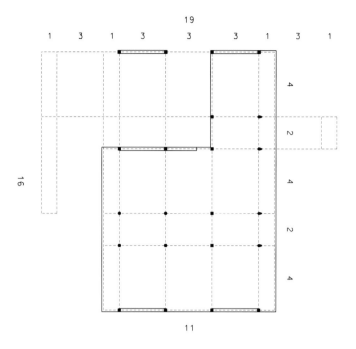

PIANO NOBILE

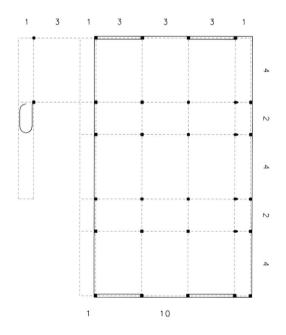

GROUND FLOOR

FIGURE 5 HILDNER © 2005 TAPP. Diagrams of the schematic interval-structure of the Villa de Monzie/Stein's ground floor and *piano nobile* plans, showing my alternative numbering system based on doubling. Ratios that describe the primary rectangular field of the villa (north-south\east-west) are **1:3:3:3:1 \ 4:2:4:2:4**. The summary sequence is **1:2:3:4**. Unlike Rowe's diagrams, column locations and shapes are specific, and additional north-south intervals that extend into the site are also shown. (East is down.)

PYTHAGOREAN PURISM

In another text, Wittkower explains that in addition to the octave, fifth, fourth, and double octave, also inherent in the ratios 1:2:3:4 is a fifth ratio, the octave plus a fifth (1:3).[24] Moreover, according to Wittkower, three of the five ratios comprise "simple" consonances, and two comprise "compound" consonances. The simple consonances include the ratios of the octave (1:2 or 2:4), the fifth (2:3), and the fourth (3:4). The compound consonances include the double octave (1:4) and the octave plus a fifth (1:3). Thus at Garches, the fundamental ratio of the east-west dimension of the grid is the simple consonance 2:4, and, by contrast, the fundamental ratio of the north-south dimension of the grid is the compound consonance 1:3. The other three ratios function to mathematically interconnect the two dimensions of the grid— in other words, these ratios mediate the fundamental opposition between the east-west and north-south intervals, which is expressed as the simple\compound consonance, 2:4\1:3.

The chart below shows the five ratios of the Greek musical system (including the two different expressions of the octave: 1:2 and 2:4) and their corresponding relationship to the structural-spatial intervals of Le Corbusier's grid of Garches. It suggests that in order to appreciate fully the villa's harmonic schema, the cross-ratios that interconnect the east-west and north-south intervals (e.g., 2:3, the ratio of the minor east-west interval to the major north-south interval) are just as significant as the ratios that pertain to one direction of the grid only (i.e., 2:4 and 1:3). In other words, the chart reveals other aspects of the east-west\north-south interdependence that are implied by the grid's ideal 1:2:3:4 ratio system.

Wittkower also explains the difference between ratios (relation of two numbers) and proportions, which he describes as "the equality of ratios between two pairs of quantities."[25] Moreover, he distinguishes between *geometrical* proportion—1:2:4 ("the first term is to the second as the second is to the third")[26]—and *arithmetic* proportion—2:3:4 ("the second term exceeds the first by the same amount as the third exceeds the second").[27] For example, says Wittkower: **If you have two strings under identical conditions, one exactly half the length of the other, and strike them, the pitch of the shorter string is one octave above that of the longer one, i.e., the ratio 1:2 corresponds to the pitch of an octave. By halving the shorter string we get an octave above the first one, and the ratios of the two octaves can be expressed as 1:2:4.**[28]

Thus, at the Villa de Monzie/Stein the minor/short north-south interval (the cantilever, 1) and the two east-west intervals (2 and 4) comprise a geometrical proportion, 1:2:4, which represents the octave and double octave. That is, in addition to the octave relationship between the minor and major east-west intervals (2:4), the minor north-south interval (the cantilever) is in an octave relationship to the minor east-west interval (1:2), and also in a double octave relationship to the major east-west interval (1:4). Inherent in the villa's 1:2:3:4 Pythagorean schema, then, is the double assertion of both *ratios* and geometrical and arithmetic *proportions*, which combine to signify an ideal system on many levels (including the regulation of the north and south facades, as I discuss later). Wittkower sums up: **The discovery that all musical consonances are arithmetically expressible *by the ratios of the first four integers*, the discovery of the close correlation of sound, space (length of the string), and numbers must have left Pythagoras and his associates bewildered and fascinated, for they seemed to hold the key which *opened the door to unexplored regions of universal harmony*** [my emphasis].[29]

Considered in this light, the structural grid of the villa at Garches is a finely-tuned Pythagorean instrument. On one level, the grid provides an ideal system of order for Le Corbusier's circumstantial game of adding and subtracting columns and an ideal field for his play of spatial *extension* (expressed through the north-south intervals) and spatial *stasis* (an attribute of the east-west intervals), thus sustaining the

Villa de Monzie/Stein — Harmonic Ratios of the 1:2:3:4 Grid [n-s = north-south; e-w = east-west; m = meters; A = 1]					
1:2	octave	simple	minor n-s : minor e-w	1.25m : 2.50m	A:B
1:3	octave + fifth	compound	minor n-s : major n-s	1.25m : 3.75m	A:C
1:4	double octave	compound	minor n-s : major e-w	1.25m : 5.00m	A:D
2:4	octave	simple	minor e-w : major e-w	2.50m : 5.00m	B:D
2:3	fifth	simple	minor e-w : major n-s	2.50m : 3.75m	B:C
3:4	fourth	simple	major n-s : major e-w	3.75m : 5.00m	C:D

FIGURE 6 Le Corbusier, Analysis of *Composition with guitar and lantern*. (From *L'Esprit Nouveau*; original painting: oil on canvas, 1920.) In addition to organizational geometries indicated by Le Corbusier's superimposed regulating lines in black, white lines and numbers that I have added show the **1:2:3:4**-based whole number ratio system that underlies the painting's Pythagorean-Purist visual field.

dialectic of *fact* versus *implication* with respect to the villa's assertion of the cantilever.[30] On another level, the grid functions as the deep conceptual structure underlying Le Corbusier's plastic expression of Significant Form.[31] Its 1:2:3:4 system provides an *idealized structural field* or plan, in which Le Corbusier interposes, and against which he counterposes, a system of *contingent non-structural figures* and *sub-figures*—the musical forms—of his Purist architectural fugue. In fact, Le Corbusier's (and Ozenfant's) Purist paintings, such as *Composition with guitar and lantern* (Figure 6), which functioned as the laboratory for his research into form, manifest the same theme of point\counterpoint between an underlying 1:2:3:4-based mathematical ordering system and the melodic visual arrangement of figurative forms regulated by a painterly eye. Musical instruments in Le Corbusier's paintings take on added significance. The guitar, for example, in addition to various conventional meanings—art, body, solid form, landscape—signifies the presence of a harmonizing force, a civilizing, mathematical intelligence.[32] In the ontology of Le Corbusier's architectonic aesthetic system, music represents the Purist-Platonic coexistence of the sensory and the intellectual.

THE PARTHENON

MATHEMATICAL PARADIGM

Ultimately, I seem to be the first to shift consideration of the north-south organizational structure of Garches to the foreground and to realize clearly that Le Corbusier's grid represents an elegant mathematical paradigm in the classical Greek sense. Moreover, Garches, I believe, is Le Corbusier's homage to the Parthenon, the paragon of mathematically regulated form, machine-like precision, and sensory\intellectual beauty that he revered so ardently above all other buildings. In *Towards a New Architecture*, published in 1923, only a few years before he worked on Garches, Le Corbusier called the Parthenon a "pure creation of the mind."[33] And he made his tribute to the Parthenon manifest through Garches by using the device of the Greek golden section, which has been central to most architects' understanding of the villa's geometrical proportions.[34] But the tribute runs deeper. The presence of an ancient\modern Parthenon-inspired consciousness—pure, clarified, and economical—reverberates more intensely. On poetical as well as rational levels, we can associate the elegant—*unforgettable*—mathematics of Le Corbusier's plastic system with something more archetypal than the ABABA rhythm of Palladio's 16th-century Italian villa. The simple\compound **1:2:3:4** grid of Garches, and the architecture that rises from it, resonates with the musical-arithmetical syntax and aesthetic idealism of ancient Greece.[35]

Towards a New Architecture
Le Corbusier, 1923

PROPRIETE DE Mme DE MONZIE

FIGURE 7 Le Corbusier, Villa de Monzie/Stein, Garches, 1927. Axonometric of the northwest corner. © FLC 10444. (See *LCA*, vol. 3, pp. 389.)

"WE ARE NOT UNMOVED BY THE INTELLIGENCE THAT GOVERNS CERTAIN MACHINES,

PROPORTION RULED ABSOLUTELY THERE, AS ABSOLUTE MISTRESS. — LE CORBUSIER [36]

REVERSAL | DISPLACEMENT — 1\A

The authenticity of this assertion above by Le Corbusier, regarding the rigorous degree to which proportion is a conscious attribute of Garches's identity, is corroborated by looking at the 1:2:3:4-based ordering system's larger role in the design of the villa. What emerges in particular is the considerable degree to which the *north-south* intervals regulate important aspects of the composition. Le Corbusier's axonometric studies (Figure 7), which permit rare glimpses of the end elevations, hint at this. One crucial idea to which these intervals give expression in the north-south direction is the *cantilever*.

The cantilever, an iconic technological-formal device of modern architecture, plays very different roles in the Le Corbusier-Rowe numbering system and in mine. The difference arises from but ultimately transcends mathematical dissimilarities, and it is a difference that hinges on another device at once independent but in this case inseparable from the cantilever: the *module*.

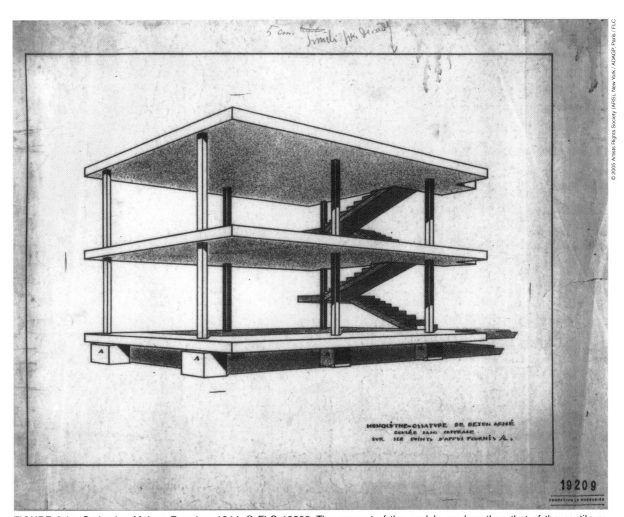

FIGURE 8 Le Corbusier, Maison Dom-ino, 1914. © FLC 19209. The concept of the module, no less than that of the cantilever, is intrinsic to the ideology of the Dom-ino system.

BY THE RIGOROUSLY CALCULATED PROPORTIONS OF THEIR COMPONENTS, BY THE

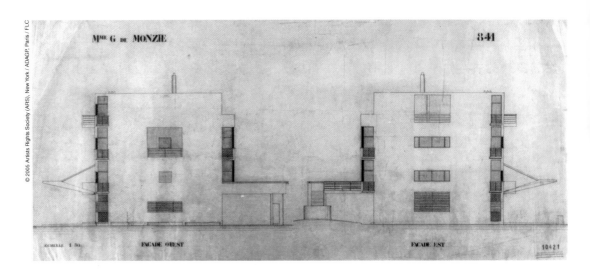

FIGURE 9 Le Corbusier, Villa de Monzie/Stein, Garches, 1927. Drawings of the west and east elevations/facades. © FLC 10421. (See *LCA*, vol. 3, p. 377.) Note the tension between the influences of Adolf Loos (Tzara House, Paris, 1925–26; upper left, opposite page) and Gerrit Rietveld (Schroder House, Utrecht, 1924; upper right, opposite page), that is, the tension between the inward, *centripetal* forces of Loosian neoclassicism (stasis, symmetry, unity, autonomy, centralization) and the outward, *centrifugal* counterforces of de Stijl modernism (dynamism, asymmetry, fragmentation, contingency, peripheralization)—counterforces, ultimately, that charge Garches's self-contained Loosian-like facades with lateral extension beyond the frame and connect the building to the larger spatial continuum of the site. This tension underlies Le Corbusier's control of the solid\void (full\empty) compositional structure.

In the 1:2:3:4 system, unlike the Le Corbusier-Rowe numbering system, the cantilever and the module are coherently related. In other words, with respect to the problem of how to identify which structural interval of the grid is primary (generative)—that is, which interval ought to be assigned the significant number, 1—the two systems clearly differ on conceptual and pragmatic levels as much as they do on the level of mathematical expression. In the Le Corbusier-Rowe numbering system, the minor east-west interval, 2.5 meters, is the starting point, 1. This 1, however, does not represent A, as one might logically anticipate. Instead, 1 represents B (i.e., B=1). Nonetheless (illogic aside), the formulations that represent the conventional, Le Corbusier-Rowe–based view of the grid can be expressed as follows (east-west\north-south): 2:1:2:1:2 \ ½:1½:1½:1½:½ = ABABA \ CDDDC.

But in the **1:2:3:4** system, the north-south cantilever interval, **1.25 meters**, is the starting point, **1**. Which means that this interval can function—whereas the minor 2.5-meter east-west interval (1 in the Le Corbusier-Rowe system) cannot—as the irreducible basic unit, or module, of which the other intervals are whole multiple moduli. Moreover, appropriately, **1=A**. Thus, the resulting numerical and alphabetical formulations, splendidly rational, are as follows (north-south\east-west): **1:3:3:3:1 \ 4:2:4:2:4 = ACCCA \ DBDBD (A=1).**[37]

CANTILEVER | MODULE

While the cantilever's arithmetical identity (½) is under-prioritized in the hierarchy of the Le Corbusier-Rowe numbering system, and thus the cantilever's connection to the concept of a module is undeveloped, Rowe's essay does make clear that the cantilever exerts a unique shaping force on the architecture of Garches and that it is the principal device whereby Garches is differentiated conceptually (and therefore mathematically) from Palladio's Malcontenta.[38] In fact, were it not for Le Corbusier's introduction of this disruptive device, the north-south and east-west intervals of the grid might well have been identical, as early studies show.[39]

Though Rowe never made an explicit connection between cantilever and module, he hinted at the connection in various ways. For example, he used the term "modular grid" in the original 1947 article.[40] Significantly, however, he did not employ the term in the 1976 edition. Also, he chose as the lead illustration for the 1947 essay Le Corbusier's iconic perspective of the Dom-ino system, but this illustration is downplayed in the 1976 edition. Moreover, as the caption that accompanies the illustration in the 1947 article indicates,[41] Rowe evoked the Dom-ino primarily to make the point that the cantilever is an expression of the liberating potential of concrete frame technology. Consider, however, that the concept of the module, no less than that of the cantilever, is intrinsic to the ideology of the Dom-ino system, as Eleanor Gregh

Adolf Loos, Tzara House, Paris | 1925–26

Gerrit Rietveld, Schroder House, Utrecht | 1924

has explained.[42] It then becomes clear, in ways Rowe's essay does not elucidate, that these two ideas, cantilever and module, are interwoven in Le Corbusier's compound Dom-ino system at Garches. The name *Dom-ino* is a reference to both the Latin word for house (*domus*) and the game (viewed in plan, the Dom-ino structure, with its six columns regularly deployed in the rectangular field of the concrete floor and roof slabs, looks like a domino piece). Le Corbusier loved the cars, planes, and domestic industrial objects or Purist *object-types* of modern culture—everything that evoked the machine-like precision and mathematical absolutes of form that he associated with the Parthenon and ancient Greece. Garches reflects this unique looking-back\looking-forward frame of mind. Le Corbusier conflated enduring principles of ancient Greece (the ideal) with new realities of modern industrialization (the practical) and made of the house a dialectical game, one that operates on numerous levels and involves advanced form-space relationships inspired by his paintings. And the rigor of the game is supported by mathematical exactitude. Le Corbusier employed the cantilever/module not only as an *ideal compositional regulator*, but also as a *practical constructional regulator*. One and one-quarter (**1.25**) meters equals approximately four feet (4'–1-7/32", to be precise), which is the standard dimensional module that undergirds much American architecture, evident in contemporaneous work of Wright and Schindler, as well as in construction practice today.

In other words, in simplest terms, Garches is based on a conventional 4-foot planning module. Expressed in feet (approximately), the ratio sequences (north-south\east-west) of the structural intervals are **4:12:12:12:4 \ 16:8:16:8:16**, and the summary sequence is **4:8:12:16**.

In addition to functioning as the mathematical basis or datum for the "universal harmony" of the ideal 1:2:3:4 grid, this 1.25-meter/4-foot module also functions as a dimensional datum. The module's double role provides the basis for both the systematic structuring of significant compositional moves and for the standardization of the building's components. On the one hand, the cantilever/module is the basis for Le Corbusier's rigorous mathematical organization of the horizontal field (i.e., the plan), which is apparent in various aspects such as: (a) the width of the "extra" interval of the cantilevered terrace and stair at the back of the villa and the subdivisions of the entrance canopy at the front, as noted earlier; (b) the projections of the other principal features of the front facade—namely, the central loggia at the attic floor and the balcony of the *piano nobile* above the secondary entrance, discussed later; and (c) the structuring of the site plan—what I call the *Extended Field*, or larger landscape of architectural production, also discussed later. On the other hand, the cantilever/module is the basis for his standardization of important building systems. In addition to the structural system, the glazing system is also clearly regulated by this module, as is seen, for example, in the sixteen windows of the *fenêtres en longueur* of the front facade (16 windows at 1.25 meters each = 20 meters) and, correspondingly, in the similar window units of the *fenêtres en longueur* of the garden facade (see p. 48).[43]

CONSISTENCY OF THEIR MOVEMENT; THEY ALMOST SEEM LIKE PROJECTIONS OF NATURAL LAWS.

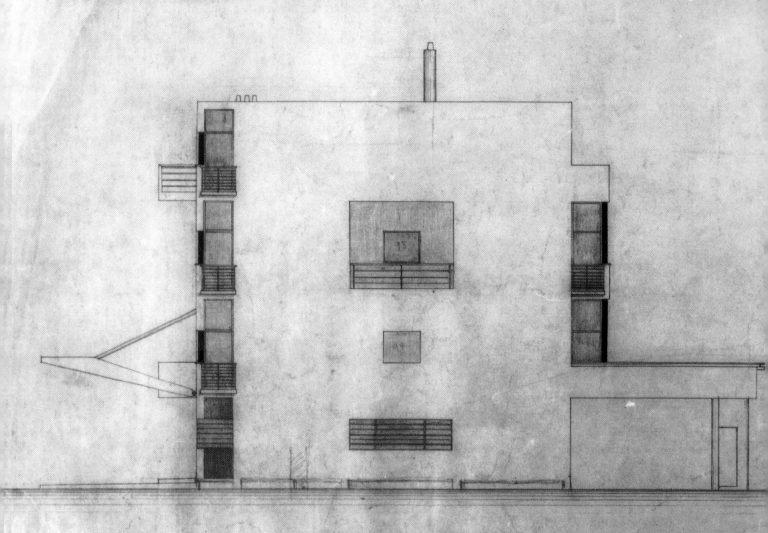

Mme G de MONZIE

ECHELLE 1 50   FACADE OUEST

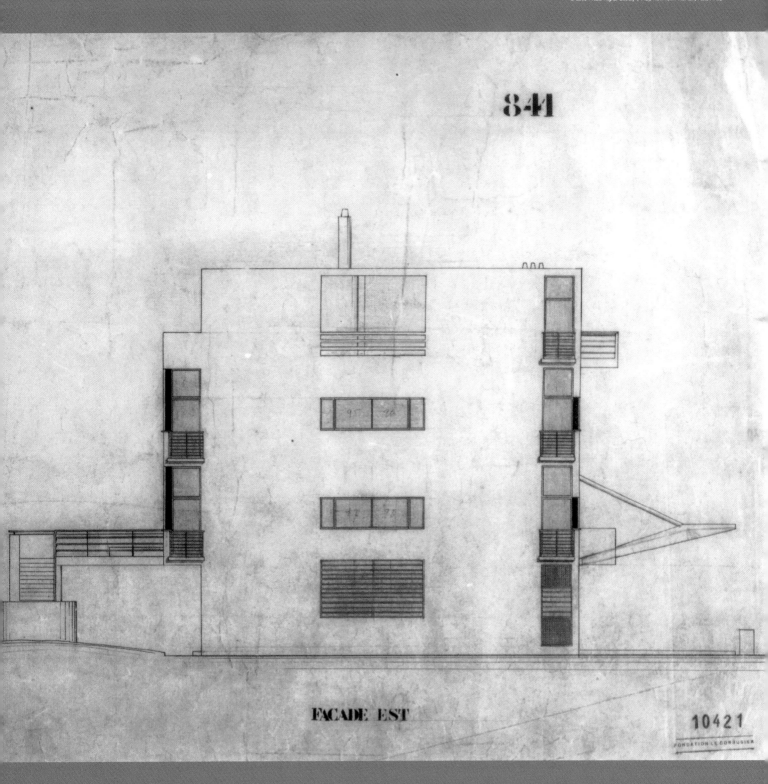

841

FACADE EST

10421

FONDATION LE CORBUSIER

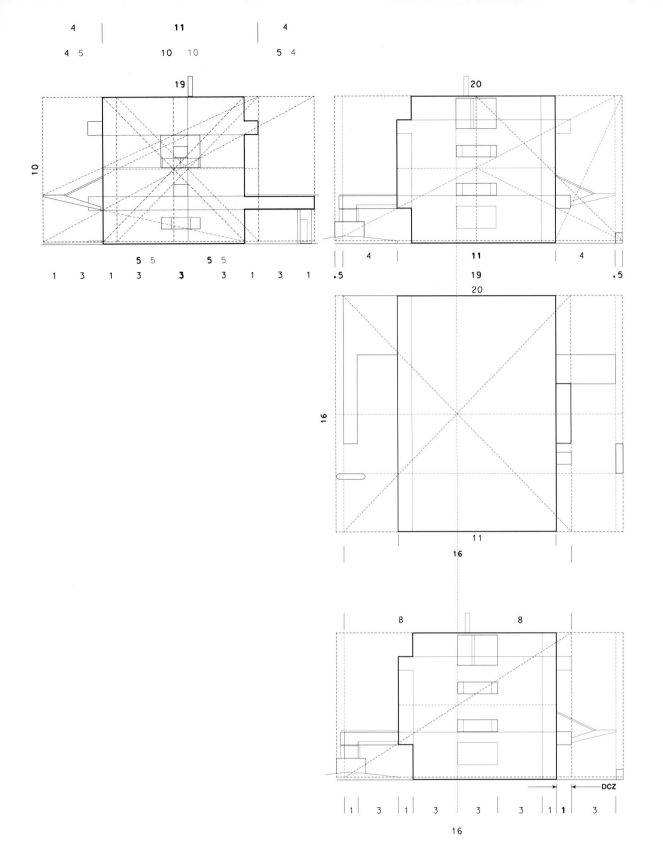

FIGURE 10 (top left) HILDNER © 2005 TAPP. Schematic diagram of the Villa de Monzie/Stein's west elevation.

FIGURE 11 (top right and middle) HILDNER © 2005 TAPP. Schematic diagrams of the Villa de Monzie/Stein's east elevation and plan (east is down).

FIGURE 12 (bottom right) HILDNER © 2005 TAPP. Schematic diagram of the Villa de Monzie/Stein's east elevation, showing what I call the **Double-Cantilever Zone** (DCZ).

OF PERFECTION." —*After Cubism*, Amédée Ozenfant and Charles-Edouard Jeanneret

It is important to note the significance of the hierarchical tension that exists between the cantilever/module (1) and the major east-west interval (4) in the new numbering system. In terms of their real dimensions, the former (1.25 meters) may be equivalent to the base module, but the latter (5 meters) has no less practical or theoretical significance to Le Corbusier's work. In terms of their interval designations, 1 may be numerically rudimental, but 4 rivals it symbolically and practically. They are physically juxtaposed at the corners of the facades and also conceptually juxtaposed at many levels, which numerous examples reveal.[44] If the cantilever interval is numerically fractional (1.25) and resides at the edge, the other is numerically whole (5) and asserts itself principally at the center. Research by others has shown that the middle 5-meter bay of the north facade, in particular, was conceptually dominant for Le Corbusier.[45] This edge\center opposition between 1 and 4 may be understood as a sign of the dialectical tension between classicism and modernism, which Rowe identified as one of Garches's transcendent themes. Consistent with Rowe's observation, a fundamental tension exists between the classical, rectangular figure of the facades that are governed by the east-west intervals (2 and 4, the even numbers) and the modernist, idiosyncratic figure of the elevations that are governed by the north-south intervals (1 and 3, the odd numbers).[46] The latter, however, are no less rigorously defined mathematically, as I show in the following analysis.

NORTH – SOUTH READINGS

Because post-Rowe scholars have focused on the east-west intervals of the grid, the end elevations have received little attention (Figure 9 and pp. 32, 33). Yet it is clear that the matrix of intervals that regulates the proportional composition of the end elevations (and the corresponding proportional composition of the plan from front to back) is meticulously developed. There is, with respect to the composition running north-south, a tension between two overall interval readings, and each reveals a multiplicity of rigorous geometric events.

The first overall reading focuses on the 11-moduli–wide by 10-moduli–high vertical field of the primary volume (Figure 10). The width of this field is defined by the five major structural intervals, 1:3:3:3:1. The windows and various sub-figures within the windows are centered within this field, which implies a centripetal organizational force. The basic symmetry is dimensionally maintained (though a countervailing centrifugal force is introduced) when the extensions to the primary volume—extensions such as the terrace and stair to the south and the suspended entrance canopy to the north—are considered. The extended field is 19 moduli wide by 10 moduli high. The 19 moduli proceed in the sequence **1:3–1:3:3:3:1–3:1**, the readings being identical whether read from north to south or from south to north. Within this dimensional symmetry, a subtle, asymmetrical tension is implied by the presence of overlapping 10:10 squares that help to organize architectural events within the 11-moduli–wide by 10-moduli–high vertical field of the main volume. The width of one 10:10 square is defined by the north and south facades of the ground floor. The width of the other 10:10 square is shifted one module/interval to the south to align with the south facade of the *piano nobile* level. These squares set up a tension with the underlying centripetal **4:11:4** emphasis (an emphasis of symmetry) within the overall 19-moduli width of the vertical field. Two counter-readings are introduced that establish the presence of centrifugal tension within the plastic structure of the vertical field: **4:10:5** and **5:10:4**, reading from north to south along the east or west elevations. Furthermore, the overlapping 10:10 squares help to illuminate the devices of geometric construction that Le Corbusier used to organize the figures and sub-figures of the vertical field. Each 10:10 square has a different centerline from the centerline of the 11:10 rectangular field of the principal volume. Le Corbusier has employed all three of these centerlines as interdependent organizing devices. For example, the center of the south-shifted 10:10 square is marked by the north edge of the proposed vent stack on the roof. This is an example of Le Corbusier's use of visible, physical traces to mark the invisible geometric construct of his fields, a device that he employs in other significant ways at the villa. The vent stack contributes to the system of asymmetrical counterforces that operate within the overall dimensionally-symmetric **19:10** vertical field. The vent stack and terrace pull to the south, and the suspended entrance canopy and balcony projections pull to the north. The diagrams show how the sub-diagonals of the overlapping squares govern the integral geometric relationship of the suspended entrance canopy. Within this first overall reading, Le Corbusier provides further evidence of his obsession with proportional rigor in the unexecuted details of his design. One observes his clear intention to extend the **19:16** ratio in plan and the 19:10 ratio in elevation to their more stable, satisfying resolutions (Figure 11). Two minor elements at the northern and southern boundaries that are each equivalent to an additional ½ module are evident in the axonometric drawings and elevations. Functioning in a way similar to the vent stack on the roof, these two elements mark the geometric limits of a composition that Le Corbusier stretches to 20 moduli from front to back. Thus, significantly: (a) the ratio of depth to height in elevation, **20:10**, describes a double square, which is not only important to Le Corbusier as a geometric figure in its own right but also echoes the 4:2 ratio of the alternating rhythm of the north-south intervals; and (b) the ratio of the depth to width in plan, **20:16** (5:4), coincides numerically with the metric dimension of the cantilever/module, 1.25.

(Le Corbusier) | October 15, 1918

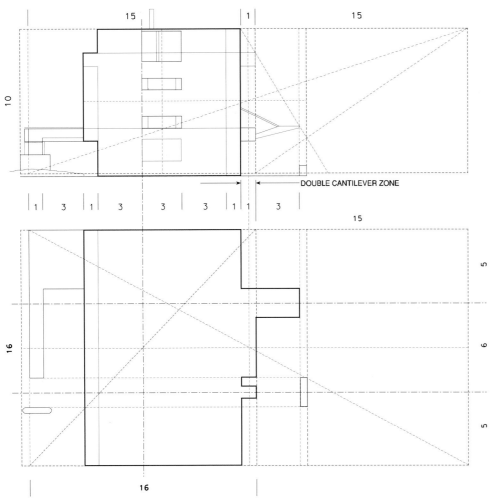

FIGURE 13 HILDNER © 2005 TAPP. Schematic diagrams of the Villa de Monzie/Stein's east elevation and plan, showing the figural and proportional interlock of the villa (solid) and entry court (void). (East is down.)

FIGURE 14 Le Corbusier, Villa de Monzie/Stein, Garches, 1927. View of the interior. © FLC L1(10)70. (See *Oeuvre complète* 1910–1929, p. 148.) Note the spatial significance of the cantilever zone (the villa's mathematical datum: **1**)—a slot of space behind the north facade (right edge of the photo).

DOUBLE-CANTILEVER ZONE

If the first overall interval reading of the east and west elevations is defined fundamentally by the boundary of symmetry around the main volume (a symmetry organized around the center windows within the 19:10 vertical rectangular field), the second overall interval reading is defined fundamentally by a similar boundary of asymmetry, which shifts attention to the edge, as defined by the north facade. This shift of focus occurs if the balconies that project from the front facade, rather than the entrance canopy, define the northern boundary. The balconies, which are cantilevered an additional module beyond the cantilevered strip, define what I call the *double-cantilever zone* (Figure 12). Thus, while the boundaries of the plan define a rectangle of elusive significance, whose ratio of depth to width is 19:16 (unless resolved to 20:16, as described above), the double-cantilever zone establishes an alternate outer boundary of what is revealed to be the inherent 16:16 square of the composition. In section, these same boundaries define a golden rectangle, 16 moduli wide by 10 moduli high. The module of the double-cantilever zone is the dominant interval of the 16 moduli that proceed from south to north (at the east elevation) in the sequence **1:3–1:3:3:3:1–1**. The diagram shows how Le Corbusier used the geometry of this 16:10 rectangular field to organize additional elevational moves. The centerline of this asymmetrical field coincides with the south edge of the central windows, creating the basic subdivision of 8 moduli to the south, which is predominantly void, and 8 moduli to the north, which is predominantly solid. While the double-cantilever zone establishes the significant edge of this essentially centrifugal reading of the elevation, it also establishes a new geometric center of an opposing centripetal reading. This new center is between the solid of the house and the void of the threshold space in front of the house, as defined by the boundary of the parking court. The double-cantilever zone is the territory of overlap that defines a double square in plan and a double golden rectangle in section[47] (Figure 13). In plan, therefore, the boundaries of the horizontal field have now been expanded to a rectangle 31 moduli by 16 moduli (**31:16**). And in elevation, the boundaries of the vertical field have been expanded to a rectangle 31 moduli by 10 moduli (**31:10**). Thus, the intervals that define the reading from south to north (in plan and in elevation) along the sequence of 31 moduli are as follows: **1:3–1:3:3:3:1–1–15**. Other than the ground-floor entrance terrace, which is a two-dimensional surface, the entrance canopy is the one element that penetrates the double-cantilever zone and bridges the two realms.

TEXT & DRAWINGS | PHOTOS

Graphic, narrative, and mathematical information relating to the end elevations of the Villa de Monzie/Stein is all but nonexistent in the chapter on Garches in Le Corbusier's *Oeuvre complète* 1910–1929. Yet the cantilever, the principle plastic expression to which the end elevations give rise, is everywhere apparent in the photographs. Take for example the view Le Corbusier provides of the interior behind the north facade (a variation of Figure 14). Most significantly, compare the juxtaposition of the two photographs that introduce the chapter (see opposite page, lower image).[48] The left photograph (a variation of Figure 15) declares the calm authority of the contracted frontal plane, organized according to the stable alternation of east-west intervals. The right photograph (similar to Figure 1) countervails. It proclaims the dynamic, disruptive power of the **cantilever/double-cantilever** in its various expressions and the latent authority of the north-south section (whose presence is also implied by the deep space of the left photograph) from which it originates. As I see it, Le Corbusier sets the stage for a dialectical drama that plays out in subsequent pages of the chapter between text and drawings on the one hand and photographs on the other. The primacy of the east-west intervals is manifested unequivocally in the former. By contrast, the significance of the north-south intervals, which is essentially unacknowledged in text and drawings, asserts itself in the photographic record. As if to underscore the odd, almost mischievous balance this produces and hint at where an essential key to the ideal mathematics that govern the project ultimately is to be found, Le Corbusier exaggerated the difference in scale between these two initial images: He made the right photograph three times larger than the left.

FIGURE 15 Le Corbusier, Villa de Monzie/Stein, Garches, 1927. View of the site threshold. © FLC L1(10)13. (See *Oeuvre complète* 1910–1929, p. 141; as per reproduction below.) Note the deep space\shallow space tension defined by the east-west surface of the villa (background) and the north-south volume of the gatehouse (foreground). As at the Acropolis, where the Propylea function as the threshold to the Parthenon, so too the gatehouse serves the same purpose—visually, spatially, ceremonially—at Garches. On the one hand, the space between the two structures (middle ground) defines an outdoor room, which functions as the Villa's forecourt; on the other hand, optical forces visually conflate their surfaces and, as in a Purist painting, the space between collapses, thus unifying the plastic scheme.

VILLA à GARCHES 1927

Villa à Garches. L'entrée dans la propriété

Entrée et garage

141

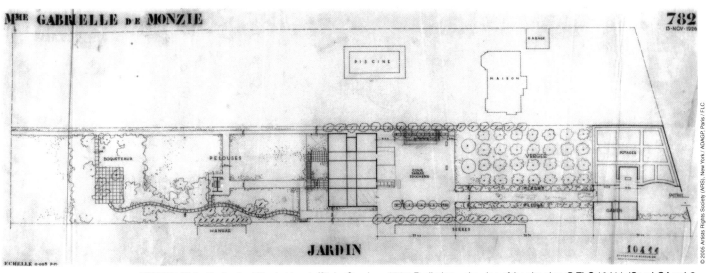

FIGURE 16 Le Corbusier, Villa de Monzie/Stein, Garches, 1927. Preliminary drawing of the site plan. © FLC 10411. (See *LCA*, vol. 3, p. 370.) (East is down.) Note, in addition to the placement of the villa at the center of the site (with respect to the north-south longitudinal axis), the early experiment with an ABA-based rhythm of the structural-spatial intervals in *both* directions of the grid (see note 39).

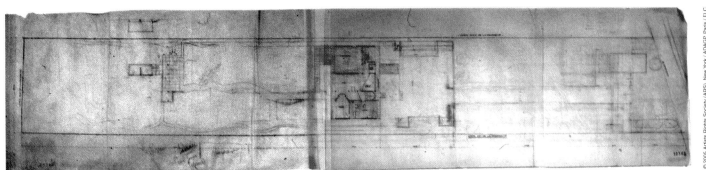

FIGURE 17 Le Corbusier, Villa de Monzie/Stein, Garches, 1927. Preliminary drawing of the site plan © FLC 10565. (See *LCA*, vol. 3, p. 444.) (East is down.) Note, again, the placement of the villa at the center of the site (with respect to the north-south longitudinal axis).

IN THIS CASE, MATHEMATICS PROVIDE SOME COMFORTING TRUTHS: ONE LEAVES ONE'S WORK WITH THE CERTITUDE THAT THE EXACT RESULT HAS BEEN REACHED. — LE CORBUSIER [49]

THE EXTENDED FIELD or larger landscape of architectural production

Le Corbusier's preoccupation with the idea of mathematics as the cabalistic key[50] that locks an architecture into the harmony of the cosmos makes itself manifest on other levels at the Villa de Monzie/Stein. It appears that he may well have employed the 1:2:3:4-based ratio\proportional system to regulate the north-south intervals of the deep space of the entire site (Figures 16 and 17), including the important relationship of the villa (the main house) to the gatehouse.

Using Werner Seligmann's field-measurements and field-measured site plan as my point of departure[51] (Figure 18), I conjecture that the site plan of Garches represents an idealized set of relationships (Figure 19). Here are several observations.

First, Le Corbusier employs the device of *displacement*—effected through parallel axes and lateral and diagonal shifts—to establish a spatial tension between the center of the villa and the center of the site, thus revealing that their interrelationship is the result of rigorous calculation. The villa's north-south centerline is shifted 1 module to the west relative to the longitudinal site centerline, which falls at the three-quarter point of the 4-module central bay (Le Corbusier marks this by a subtle secondary move on the facade). And if, as I conjecture, the villa's east-west centerline is similarly shifted relative to the transverse site-centerline,[52] in this case 1.5 modules to the north (and thus falling along an actual structural line), then this double shift establishes a strategically located 6-module (4+2, east-west) by 6-module (3+3, north-south) "X" that rather clearly marks the center of the site. This "X"—a 6:6 square whose boundaries are spatially significant within the organization of the *piano nobile* plan—establishes a dynamic, precisely delimited asymmetrical condition of center within the interior of the villa.

Second, the related issue of the inequality between the villa's east and west property-line setbacks is also the result of obvious mathematical calculation. Although the actual width of the site is dimensionally insufficient to realize the intention completely (and zoning requirements complicated the matter),[53] the 4 and 2 intervals seem clearly intended to extend beyond the villa's end walls to define these setbacks as well.

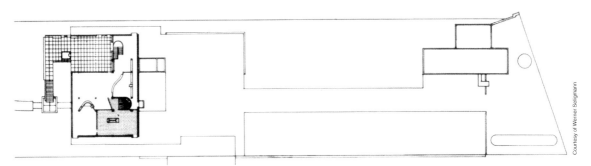

FIGURE 18 Werner Seligmann's drawing of the Villa de Monzie/Stein's partial site plan, which is based on his field measurements, shows the *piano nobile* level. (East is down.) Though Seligmann's full drawing does not show the entire site, it includes slightly more of the southern part of the site than is reproduced here. See notes 47 and 51.

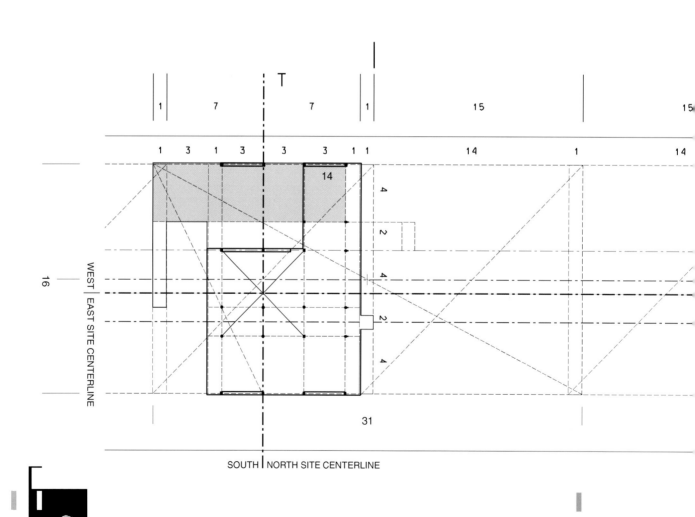

1   7   7   1   15   15

1   3   1   3   3   3   1   1   14   1   14

14

4

2

4

2

4

16

WEST | EAST SITE CENTERLINE

31

SOUTH | NORTH SITE CENTERLINE

Knight's Move

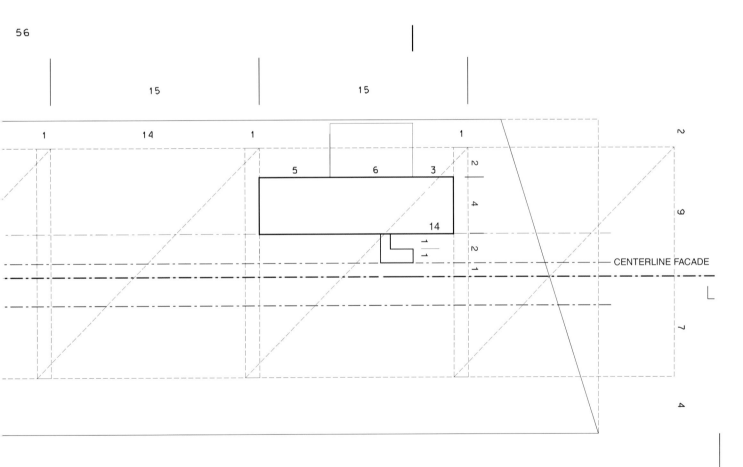

FIGURE 19 _GARCHES CHESSBOARD HILDNER © 2005 TAPP. Diagram of the Villa de Monzie/Stein's partial site plan (*piano nobile* level of the villa), showing the positioning of the villa at the geometric center of the site along the longitudinal axis (**L** = **L**ongitudinal Site Axis; **T** = **T**ransverse Site Axis) and the ***idealized*** mathematics and alignments of what I call the **Extended Field**, or larger landscape of architectural production. The principle site strategy involves a Synthetic-Cubist concept that I call the **breakaway move**—specifically, the **Knight's Move**, because the piece that breaks away simulates **the diagonal movement of a knight on a chessboard**. The formal-spatial device of the breakaway move underlies the Villa's mathematically correlated (4x14 moduli) relationship between villa (main house) and gatehouse; see Figure 20.

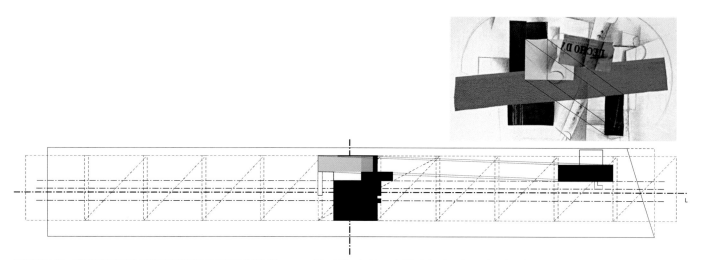

FIGURE 20 _ SITE STRATEGY HILDNER © 2005 TAPP. Diagram of the Villa de Monzie/Stein's site plan, showing the positioning of the villa at the geometric center of the site along the longitudinal axis (**L** = **L**ongitudinal Site Axis; **T** = **T**ransverse Site Axis); see Figure 19. (East is down.) Also shown is the Braque-Picasso–like Synthetic-Cubist relationship (i.e., the solid\void, figure\field relationship) between the villa (main house) and the gatehouse. My diagram illustrates Le Corbusier's major form-space tactic on the **site chessboard**: what I call the **breakaway move** (specifically, the **Knight's Move**, because the piece that breaks away simulates **the diagonal movement of a knight in chess**)—a subtractive device that produces a positive form and a corresponding negative space (and creates as well a space between the two conditions). Various permutations of the breakaway move could be diagrammed relative to the main house and gatehouse (for example, the gatehouse could be regarded as subtracted from the top floor of the main house; see Fig. 7). And other expressions of the subtractive\additive breakaway move that have nothing to do with the gatehouse weave through the composition of the main house.

Third, another example of the authority of the longitudinal site-centerline to organize important physical phenomena within the matrix of the site is underscored by the centerline's co-linearity with the west edge of the driveway and gatehouse portico. This provides another example of the thematic play of the edge\center opposition intrinsic to the project. It also signals Le Corbusier's use of the device of a diptych-line to organize the left and right formal-spatial and processional events of the villa and its site; for example, (1) the solid form of the gatehouse to the west of the longitudinal site-centerline is counterbalanced by the void-space of the entry threshold to the east and (2) the driveway and the servants' entrance, which are axially aligned (in contrast, I believe, to what Seligmann's site plan indicates), are confined to the east side, but the longitudinal site-centerline must be crossed in order to move to the front door, which is on the west side.

Fourth, the site's arithmetical logic—the ratios that underlie the relationship of villa and entry court (Figure 13) form the basis of the site's overall metering system—has been applied to the ratios that govern the size and positioning of the gatehouse within this system. The villa and the gatehouse are numerically, and thus dimensionally, interrelated through the same simple integers, with the addition of the numbers 5 and 6 contributing to the simultaneous assertion of the independent identity of the gatehouse.

FIGURE | FIELD

The arithmetical rigor of Le Corbusier's site plan underscores the axial and figural relationships between the villa and the gatehouse. Seligmann's site plan (the basis for Figure 19) hints at a network of axial centerlines, edges, and alignments that correlate the two buildings and sustain their formal interaction. Moreover, Le Corbusier was obviously *as concerned with the space between these two solid forms as with the forms themselves*. That is, he was as concerned with the algebra of the empty space—of the outdoor room, or void—defined by the two objects as with the objects themselves. And within Le Corbusier's disciplined chess game delimiting solid and void, affinities between what I call *figure* and *field* operate on many levels. A similar ratio in plan (**7:2**) governs the small figure of the principal rectangular block of the gatehouse (**14:4**) and the field of the large space that extends to the gatehouse portico from the villa's front facade (**56:16**). Of the two volumes that comprise the gatehouse, the subordinate side volume is a 4:6 rectangle in plan, and may be thus easily understood as a partial reciprocal figure to the void of the villa's southwest terrace (this void is in lateral alignment with the villa's 6:6 square site-center described above). There are various readings, such as the one shown here (Figure 20), by which the principal volume of the gatehouse, 14:4, may also be conceptualized as a fragment that has been subtracted from the solid volume of the villa. This idea, whereby the gatehouse is viewed as a cutout, separated from the villa and displaced on the site—the device I call the **breakaway move**—is one that I believe Le Corbusier learned from post-1911 Synthetic Cubist experiments, such as those by Braque (Figure 21), who was equally mathematically-minded in his organization of the visual field.[54]

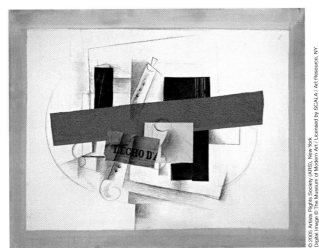

FIGURE 21 (left) Braque, Georges (1882–1963) © ARS, NY. *Still Life with Tenora* (formerly called *Clarinet*). 1913. Pasted paper, oil, charcoal, chalk, and pencil on canvas. 37½ x 47¼ in. Nelson A. Rockefeller Bequest. (947.1979). Interlocking cut-figures in Braque's Synthetic-Cubist game of figure\field reciprocity create a visual-spatial realm of the sort that influenced Le Corbusier's aesthetic research. The three darkest fragments (vertical rectangle, upper left; and two-part reverse "C," right of center) correlate through a technique I call the **breakaway move**—specifically, the **Knight's Move** (a knight moves diagonally on a chessboard). In other words, think of the reverse "C" as an eroded rectangle (under the wide wood-grain band) whose missing piece broke away to the left and up. (Opposite page inset somersaults the collage and shows guidelines to make the point.) The subtractive breakaway move acts not only as a form-making device, but also as a **space-making device**—and underlies the positive-negative relationships at play in various ways at Garches, including the relationship between villa (main house) and gatehouse. (See pp. 52–53 for further illustration of these principles.)

FIGURE 22 (right) Le Corbusier, Villa de Monzie/Stein, Garches, 1927. View of the south facade. Note the Braque connection.

For all its apparent autonomy, the Villa de Monzie/Stein, within its adopted aesthetic system of formal moves, is as much about *relationships* as it is about *objects*. The villa and gatehouse are two elements of one site, fragments of a larger interdependent whole, whose figure\field counterpoints and interlocks are mathematically disciplined through the syncopated rhythms of simple whole-number relationships.

S : M : L : XL[55]

The house's position at the center of the site makes it a diptych-like mediator between front and back landscapes. Le Corbusier believed that "the exterior is always an interior."[56] This gives rise to a reading of the Villa de Monzie/Stein in which the entire site becomes "building" (and the entire building, "site")—a "building" that is primarily a void, and whose roof is therefore primarily not material, but celestial (sky). Le Corbusier's famous sketch of an early design at Garches (see page 12) shows how important building\site reciprocity was to him. It conveys how he conceived of architecture as much as a *space-definer* as a *space-occupier*. In the site-as-building\building-as-site scheme of the Villa as built, the front (northern) and back (southern) landscapes are the two biggest rooms. If the southern landscape is the **extra-large** outdoor room, by implication extending infinitely to the horizon, then the northern landscape—the "entry hall" to the villa from the street—is the compressed **large** outdoor room. The villa's roof terrace functions as the **medium** outdoor room and its *piano nobile* south terrace as the **small** one (Figure 22): four outdoor rooms, four "gardens." Thus, the Villa de Monzie/Stein presents a clear homologous relationship between the mathematical and conceptual ordering of space inside and outside, and the idea of *four*—a sequence of four numbers, **1:2:3:4**, and four scales, **S:M:L:XL**—is an important part of its poetic logic.

1:1 SYMMETRY — 1:2 ASYMMETRY

Le Corbusier's regulation of the site heightens perception of the underlying devices of symmetry and asymmetry—devices that represent the formal-spatial expression of the more general dialectical concept sameness\difference. The ratio **1:1** is the ratio of symmetry, of equality. Relationships that are 1:1 are based on division into halves. The 1:1 ratio represents the equal or diptychal condition of the split-screen.[57] It is the underlying principle of centering. The ratio **2:1** or 4:2, Le Corbusier's favorite proportional device, is the fundamental ratio of asymmetry, of inequality. Relationships that are 2:1 are based on division into thirds. The 2:1 ratio represents the basic *un*equal condition of the split-screen. It is the underlying principle of decentering. Ratios that are **3:1** (division into quarters), **4:1** (division into fifths), and so on, extend the series (which is infinite) of clearly definable conditions of asymmetry and attendant split-screens. These are the ratios that are at play in Le Corbusier's masterful control of the complex symmetries and asymmetries—the complex centerings and decenterings—of the Villa de Monzie/Stein's composition.

Le Corbusier, Villa de Monzie/Stein, Garches, 1927. North/street-side facade. © FLC L1(10)24. (See *LCA*, vol. 3, pp. 367.)

Le Corbusier, Villa de Monzie/Stein, Garches, 1927. South/garden-side facade. (See *Oeuvre complète* 1910–1929, p. 46.)

ALL THE ELEMENTS OF THE FACADE ARE IN HARMONY WITH ONE ANOTHER. PRECISION HAS CREATED SOMETHING FINAL, SHARP, TRUE, UNCHANGEABLE AND PERMANENT, WHICH IS THE ARCHITECTURAL MOMENT. — Le Corbusier[58]

MODULE | GOLDEN NUMBER

Finally, attention may be directed anew to the issue of Le Corbusier's regulation of the Villa de Monzie/Stein's north and south facades. It is generally recognized that these facades represent Le Corbusier's early attempt to posit a dualistic mathematical proportional system. In its mature stage, this system, as Wittkower and others have observed, formed the basis for Le Corbusier's *Modulor* system, which he published in 1948.[59] Fundamentally, the system relied on ideas that are revealed in the renowned drawings of the villa's facades (Figure 2). In these drawings, Le Corbusier asserted the combined principles of the module, the golden number, and the regulating line. The first two principles were important during the design of the project. The diagonal regulating lines were added after the project was designed.[60] Moreover, in his use of the golden number, Le Corbusier suppressed its essential incommensurable identity (1.618…) and emphasized its rationalized commensurable approximation, 8:5 (1.6). This enabled the two antithetical ideas—the module and the golden number—to be harmoniously combined. I maintain, therefore, that the mathematical substructure of the Villa de Monzie/Stein is based principally, if not exclusively, on whole-number relationships. By using the device of the golden number approximation, Le Corbusier was able to ensure that the moduli were combined in such a way so as to be proportionally, and therefore culturally, significant on a larger level. Thus, the moduli have not only their own intrinsic numerical significance (the first four integers 1,2,3,4), but they also combine to form, approximately, the proportions of a geometrical figure (a golden-rectangle, both as three-dimensional solid form and as two-dimensional planar surface) that has its own universally resonant, honorific meaning.

      Wittkower identifies the larger philosophical significance of Le Corbusier's dialectical system, which his pre-*Modulor* research at the villa at Garches represents: **. . . two different classes of proportion, both derived from the Pythagorean-Platonic world of ideas, were used during the long history of European art. . . . The Middle Ages favoured Pythagorean-Platonic geometry, while the Renaissance and Classical periods preferred the numerical, i.e., the arithmetical side of that tradition.**[61]

The arithmetical\geometrical dialectic was central to the philosophical structure of Le Corbusier's mathematical logic. At Garches, it is given simplified expression through his rationalized, whole-number module\golden number system. Moreover, in the end, the theme of the dialectic, on a deeper level, extends to the role of the module itself. I have discovered that the module has a *dual* identity. It operates simultaneously and interdependently as part of **two 1:2:3:4-based ratio systems**, as well as in conjunction with the golden number's whole-number approximation (16:10 in my numbering system). This, I believe, underlies the composition of the Villa de Monzie/Stein's facades. A reading of Le Corbusier's own comments on the villa together with a close examination of his drawings of the facades bring this into focus.

EMPTY | FULL

Le Corbusier liked to use the terms *empty* and *full* to describe the phenomenon of alternating void\solid intervals of such things as windows (empty) and wall surface (full).[62] In fact, he used these terms to describe the facades at Garches, in a passage that reveals so much more:

> **Consider [the] drawing [of the south facade] with the details of the proportions of the villa at Garches. The *choice of proportions*, of full and empty, the determination of the height with respect to a length which in turn is dictated by the constraints of the terrain, all these are in the domain of lyrical creation. . . . However, the mind, curious and grasping, tries to get to the heart of this unrefined product in which the destiny of the work is already permanently inscribed. This search by the mind and the improvements which result from it give rise to the establishment of a mathematical order (arithmetical or geometrical) based on the "golden number," on the interplay of the perpendicular diagonals, on *arithmetical relationships involving 1, 2, 4, between the horizontal bands* [my emphasis], etc. Thus all the elements of the facade are in harmony with one another. Precision has created something final, sharp, true, unchangeable and permanent, which is the *architectural moment*.**[63]

I stumbled onto that passage late in the game. The passage validates core concepts of my argument, including my central conjecture: *Le Corbusier consciously used "arithmetical relationships involving 1, 2, 4"*—moreover, not just in plan. Imagine how I felt when I read that paragraph: **Q.E.D.!** (Q.E.D. stands for the Latin phrase *quod erat demonstrandum*, meaning "that which was to be demonstrated"; mathematicians traditionally place Q.E.D. at the end of their calculations to signal that they have definitively proved what they set out to prove.)

In that remarkable passage, Le Corbusier says that he used "arithmetical relationships" involving the rational geometrical proportion 1:2:4 to determine the heights of the empty\full bands of the north facade.[64] Which means that simple whole-number ratios regulate more than just the structural-spatial intervals of the plan and *horizontal* rhythm of the facades of the Villa de Monzie/Stein: They also regulate the empty\full *vertical* rhythm of the facades. Moreover, not only are relationships involving 1:2:4 at play, but the number 3 is obviously significant as well. In other words, I maintain, **Le Corbusier employed a 1:2:3:4-based ratio system to design Villa de Monzie/Stein's facades** (Figures 23 and 24).

THE FOURTH "SIGN" — THE *OTHER* 1

A close reading of Le Corbusier's drawing of the south facade (see Figures 2 and 24), which calls for the decoding of its mathematical "signs," is essential. Up to this point, I have identified three separate though ultimately interdependent sets of mathematical signs that Le Corbusier included on this drawing: (a) the numerical proportional system, indicated by the 2:1:2:1:2 ratio sequence, which he employed to regulate the east-west intervals of the structural system and, consequently, the *horizontal* intervals of the facades; (b) the geometric proportional system of the golden section, indicated by the alphabetical notation A and B, which he used to determine, through approximate whole-number relationships, the principal rectangular boundaries and subdivisions of the facade's two-dimensional field; and (c) the diagonal regulating lines, which he imposed on the drawing after the project was designed in order to proclaim their latent aesthetic refinement and authority. But there is a fourth sign on this drawing: the two *1*s, through which the diagonal lines cut, and which Le Corbusier placed in the "full" space of the floor structure of the upper two floors. This fourth sign—this *other* 1 that appears twice—signifies something different from the 1 that is part of the 2:1:2:1:2 ratio sequence lower in the drawing, where 1 is equivalent to 2.50 meters. This *other* 1 also signifies something different from the 1 that is part of my 1:2:3:4 numbering system, in which 1 is equivalent to 1.25 meters. I believe that this *other* 1 signifies Le Corbusier's assertion of a dimensional truth—of a dimensional *datum*: 1 meter. It refers to the actual height of each of the horizontal bands to which it is assigned in the drawing. And it is the same 1 to which Le Corbusier referred when he wrote about the "arithmetical relationships involving 1, 2, 4, between the horizontal bands." This fourth sign—1 meter—is the base module that governs the *vertical* subdivisions of the facades through a *second* 1:2:3:4-based ratio system.

THE DUAL MODULE UNIFIED-FIELD DEVICE — 1X | 1Y

The 1 (1 meter) in this second, elevation-related system, 1y:2y:3y:4y (vertical intervals of the facades), is therefore different from the 1 (1.25 meters) in the first, plan-related system, 1x:2x:3x:4x (horizontal intervals of the facades). Thus, the corresponding idealized ratio sequences, which can be represented by other permutations as well, are as follows, (x\y): south facade = **4:2:4:2:4(x) \ 2:1:2:1:2:1:2:1(y)** (Figure 23); north facade = **4:2:4:2:4(x) \ 4:1:2:1:4(y)** (Figure 24). The y-dimension (height) of the villa's facades, as well as of the villa's end elevations, is thereby composed of essentially 4 floors of 3 modules each, equalling 12 modules (12 meters).[65] Clearly, then, these two x and y systems are elegantly related mathematically through the simple ratio **5:4**. That is, since y = 1.00 meter, and x = 1.25 meters, then 1y = 4/5 of 1x, and 1x = 5/4 of 1y. That means that 5y = 4x, or, expressed another way, 5 meters = 4 times 1.25 meters. In other words, **Le Corbusier established a *dual system* of 1:2:3:4-based ratios in this villa**, and these two systems are proportional to each other by virtue of the next whole number in the sequence, 5. By employing different 1:2:3:4-based ratio systems for elevation and plan, Le Corbusier has made the double assertion that these ratio systems are simultaneously independent and dependent. He suggests, therefore, as one might expect, given the dialectical habit of his mind, that there exists in the mental, and therefore the visual, structure of the Villa de Monzie/Stein's facades a mathematically elegant quality of simplicity\complexity. Always cognizant of the relation of sameness\difference, Le Corbusier has, in effect, employed mathematics as what I call a *Unified-Field Device*; that is, he has interconnected the horizontal and vertical fields—plan and elevation—in a systematic way, without making them the same. Had he used a single 1:2:3:4-based ratio system for elevation and plan, the proportion of each of the sixteen horizontal window units that comprise the *fenêtres en longueur* of the north facade, for example, might well have been square. Inasmuch as his dominant theme is the rectangle, and that stasis, which the square represents, contradicts the expression of centrifugal extension and horizontality inherent in the anti-neoclassical counterforces of the north facade, he chose instead to use an "imperfect square," one whose ratio is **5:4**. Perhaps, in this individual window unit, which signifies the scale of the human body, Le Corbusier gives the clearest expression to the villa's *dual module ratio*. Alternately expressed as 1x\1y, **5:4**, or, in meters, 1.25:1.00, the dual module of the window sash constitutes an important mathematical "**architectural moment**." It represents a benign conflict—the elemental co-presence of the *two* 1:2:3:4-based harmonic systems that underlie the Villa de Monzie/Stein's ideal Pythagorean-Platonic mathematics.

Together these systems define an architecture that celebrates ancient and modern principles that Le Corbusier sought to integrate, an architecture at once atypical and typical: lyrical and mechanical, playful and precise, customized and standardized—and ultimately, as Le Corbusier hoped, "final, sharp, true, unchangeable and permanent."

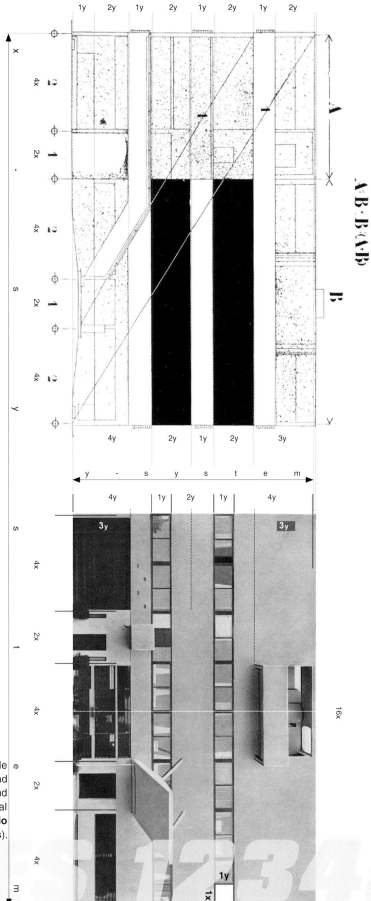

FIGURE 23 (top) and FIGURE 24 (bottom) Le Corbusier, Villa de Monzie/Stein, Garches, 1927. Drawing of the south facade (top) and view of the north façade (bottom), which I have rotated and marked (and thus abstracted/defamiliarized), showing the idealized mathematical dependence\independence of Le Corbusier's **dual 1:2:3:4-based ratio systems** that regulate the vertical field (**y=1 meter; x=1.25 meters**).

Window Module = 4:5 (1y : 1x = 1.00 : 1.25 meters)

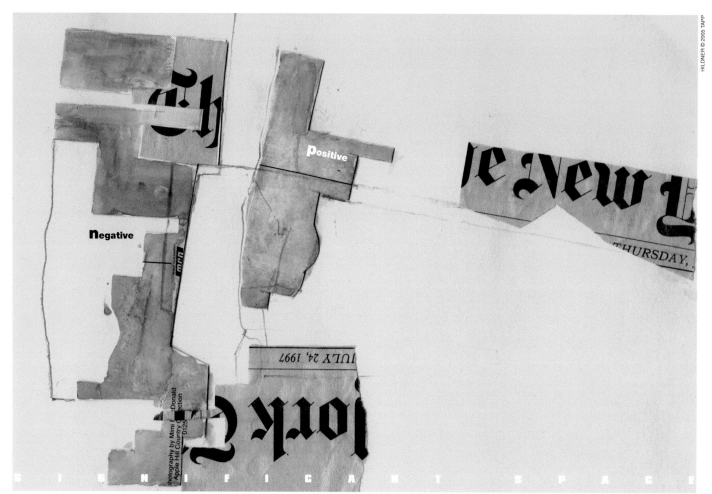

JIGSAW DESIGN. ***KNIGHT MOVES / NYT: CUT, SEPARATE, SHEAR.*** 1997. Pasted paper, gouache, and pencil on paper in spiral sketchbook. 6¼ x 9¼ in. A neo-Synthetic Cubist collage, this fractured figure\field-reciprocity study illustrates several fundamental **organizing principles** and **space-making devices** of the Braque-Picasso aesthetic system, including a simple positive-negative diagonal displacement that I call the **breakaway move**—specifically, the **Knight's Move** (a knight moves diagonally in chess). This diagonal relationship between **positive** figures and **negative** figures (as I label one pair in my collage) echoes techniques that Braque uses in *Still Life with Tenora* (aka *Clarinet*), 1913 (see p. 47). A similar relationship activates Picasso's 1912 collage *Violin* (opposite page), which includes an additional horizontal flip. In other words, Picasso turns one newspaper fragment into two fragments by a four-step procedure: cut, separate, shear, flip. Le Corbusier signals a similar awareness at Garches (more in his plans and sections than in his elevations), in which interlocking puzzle-pieces of solids and voids create a calculated figure-field system of **Significant Form** (Clive Bell's term, which he introduced in his book *Art*, 1914) and what I call SIGNIFICANT SPACE.

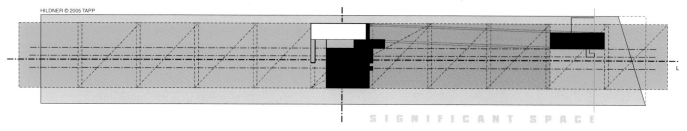

SIGNIFICANT SPACE

SEE MY ESSAY "SIGNIFICANT SPACE." https://archive.org/details/HenryTrucksPainterAncientMythsMeetModernLandscapes

Knight's Move

SEE MY ESSAY ON JIGSAW DESIGN, "MILTON AVERY: PUZZLE MASTER." https://archive.org/details/MiltonAvery-PuzzleMaster

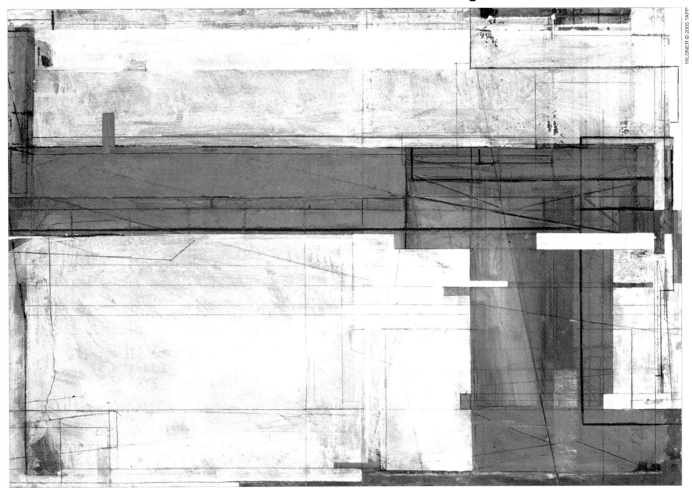

JIGSAW DESIGN. ***CHESS MOVES:*** *GARCHES STUDY _2 / DAEDALUS'S LABYRINTH.* 1997. Oil on canvas. 18 x 24 in. A combination of Knight Moves (cut, separate, shear: diagonal breakaway) and Rook Moves (cut, separate: orthogonal breakaway). Learning from Braque and Picasso (Synthetic Cubism) to create S I G N I F I C A N T   S P A C E.

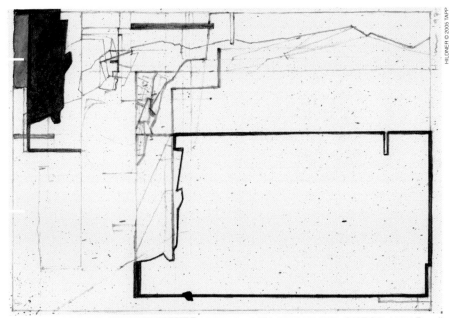

JIGSAW DESIGN. ***KNIGHT MOVES*** */ PIERO: CUT, SEPARATE, SHEAR.* 1997. Pencil and gouache on paper in spiral sketchbook. 6¼ x 9¼ in. Learning from Braque and Picasso (Synthetic Cubism) to create S I G N I F I C A N T   S P A C E.

S I G N I F I C A N T   S P A C E
Knight's Move: cut, separate, shear, flip.

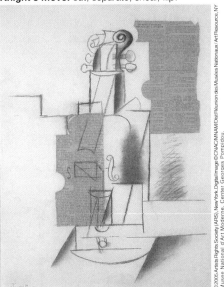

JIGSAW DESIGN. Picasso, Pablo (1881–1973) © ARS, NY. *Violin*, 1912. Charcoal and newspaper pasted on paper. 18½ x 24½ in.

Le Corbusier, Villa de Monzie/Stein, Garches, 1927. Construction photo: north/street-side facade. © FLC L1(10)8. (See *LCA*, vol. 3, pp. 367.)

Preliminary versions of this essay appeared under the title "Remembering the Mathematics of the Ideal Villa" in *86th ACSA Annual Meeting Proceedings* (1998), pp. 388–395, and in the refereed quarterly *Journal of Architectural Education* (February 1999; Vol. 52, Issue 3), pp. 143–162.

Throughout this essay, the forward slash (/) signifies analogous pairings (e.g., Monzie/Stein and cantilever/module). The backslash (\) signifies oppositional pairings (e.g., solid\void and empty\full).

The term *piano nobile* ("noble floor" in Italian) refers to the main living level of a large house; as at Garches, the *piano nobile* is typically the second floor.

1 Quoted by Daniel Naegele (source unattributed) in *Le Corbusier: Painter and Architect* (Aalborg: Architectural Magazine B, 1995), p. 83.

2 Colin Rowe, "The Mathematics of the Ideal Villa: Palladio and Le Corbusier compared," *Architectural Review* 101 (March 1947), pp. 101–104. The article has been republished three times. The first was a reprint of the original article, by the same title, in Peter Serenyi, ed., *Le Corbusier in Perspective* (Englewood Cliffs, N.J.: Prentice-Hall, 1975), pp. 46–55. This was essentially identical to the original text; however, the number, selection, and coordination of illustrations were different. The second publication was also a reprint of the original article; it appeared as "The Mathematics of the Ideal Villa," *A + U: Architecture and Urbanism* (October 1975), pp. 29–40 (English text and Japanese translation). Here, the title of the article as well as the composition and scale of the illustrations differed from both earlier editions. The third re-publication, which comprised a revised text, appeared as the title essay, "The Mathematics of the Ideal Villa," in *The Mathematics of the Ideal Villa and Other Essays* (Cambridge, Massachusetts: The MIT Press, 1976), pp. 1–27. (Since 1978, Rowe's essay has also begun to appear in foreign language translations). Although the 1976 edition includes significant revisions to the text and illustrations of the original, the essential thesis remains unaltered. I have noted any discrepancies that are pertinent to my study.

3 Numerous scholars have contributed to the popular association of Rowe with the use of alphabetical nomenclature to describe the east-west structural intervals of Le Corbusier's villa at Garches. In *Modern Architecture: A Critical History* (New York: Oxford University Press, 1980), for example, Kenneth Frampton, referring to Le Corbusier's Villa Schwob and the Villa de Monzie/Stein, writes that "both houses [are] seemingly organized about the *classic Palladian ABABA rhythm remarked on by Colin Rowe*," p. 157 (my emphasis). In the crucial essay, Rowe does of course associate Garches with the Palladian model in an indelible way. And it is worth remembering that Le Corbusier's connection to Palladio precedes Rowe's observations—as William J.R. Curtis writes: "In the 1930s he [Le Corbusier] told the South African architect, Martienssen, that he tried to recreate 'the spirit of Palladio' in the 1920s houses," Curtis, *Le Corbusier: Ideas and Forms* (Oxford: Phaidon Press Limited, 1986), pp. 80–84. But it was other scholars who ascribed to this association the so-called Palladian ABABA designation (see n. 6 below). For example, in his article on "The Grid," *Oppositions* 15/16 (Winter/Spring 1979), p. 102, Barry Maitland refers to Rowe as his point of departure and employs alphabetical notation to show how the ABABA east-west bay spacing at Garches is a special condition of Wittkower's diagram of the general Palladian geometrical pattern ABCBA where C=A. Interestingly enough, however, Wittkower employs no alphabetical designations; see Wittkower, *Architectural Principles in the Age of Humanism* (London: Alec Tiranti, 1962; reprint ed., New York: W. W. Norton & Company, 1971), p. 73. Nor, for that matter, does Palladio use them in his own *Quattro libri dell'architettura* (Venice, 1570). In fact, one must turn to Cesare Cesariano's 1521 (Como) edition of Vitruvius's *De architectura* for a systematic use of alphabetical notation to describe grid patterns.

4 Le Corbusier and Pierre Jeanneret, *Oeuvre complète*, 8 vols. (Zurich: Editions d'Architecture, 1929–1970; reprint ed. Zurich: Editions d'Architecture, 1967). See the section on the "Villa à Garches 1927" in *Oeuvre complète* 1910–1929, vol. 1, pp. 140–149.

5 In particular, Rowe described the device of the Greek golden section, especially in the 1976 edition, as an aspect of Le Corbusier's aggressive assertion of the mathematical organization of the elevations: "Le Corbusier ... carefully indicates his relationships by an apparatus of regulating lines and figures and by placing on the drawings of his elevations the ratio of the golden section, A:B=B:(A+B)," *Mathematics of the Ideal Villa*, p. 9. (See n. 34 and n. 60 below.)

6 Analysis of the scholarly record reveals the surprising degree to which a mythology has accrued to Rowe's article as well as to the grid of the Villa de Monzie/Stein at Garches itself. For example, in *The Villas of Le Corbusier: 1920–1930* (New Haven: Yale University Press, 1987), Tim Benton writes: "Ever since Colin Rowe's article 'The Mathematics of the Ideal Villa', attention has been focused on one aspect of the design [of the villa at Garches] which has been prioritized to the exclusion of other important and salient features. *Rowe emphasized* the *ABABA grid* of the Villa Stein-de Monzie, comparing it to a similar grid underlying the design of the Villa Malcontenta," p. 165 (my emphasis). First, as I have said (see n. 3 above), Rowe did not employ the formulation ABABA. Second, the designation ABABA can describe a grid only if the intervals in both directions are the same, which at Garches they are not (though he did experiment with such a scheme at one point; see n. 39). Third, Benton's assertion actually functions as an example of how other scholars, but not Rowe himself, have "emphasized the ABABA" (east-west) intervals of the grid and, consequently, how these scholars have lost sight of the north-south intervals, which I would call correlatively the CDDDC intervals; in other words, how scholars have lost sight of *the grid.* Moreover, the scholarly record reveals a different picture in regard to Benton's suggestion that the grid has received more than its share of attention. Excellent, original research on various aspects of the villa's grid has been published, not the least by Benton himself (see n. 10 below); however, while Rowe is invariably referenced in texts on the subject, in fact, themes other than the grid and the mathematical have been the primary foci of scholarship. But Benton is correct in one respect: inasmuch as Rowe's essay has been accepted as definitive, when scholars have referred to the grid of the Villa de Monzie/Stein the discussion has usually been limited to attempts to summarize Rowe's observations, focusing almost exclusively and narrowly on the iconic 2:1:2:1:2 (ABABA) comparison with Palladio's Villa Malcontenta.

7 Rowe, *Mathematics of the Ideal Villa*, p. 2.

8 Russian Formalism is central to my critical perspective, namely the desire to bring into focus a new view of a familiar object, to heighten perception of it, through the technique of *defamiliarization* or *strange-making.* Among the essential texts on the subject are Victor Shklovsky's canonical essay of 1917, "Art as Device/Technique"; see the English edition, trans. and ed. Lee T. Lemon and Marion J. Reis in *Russian Formalist Criticism: Four Essays* (Lincoln: University of Nebraska Press, 1965); and Victor Erlich, *Russian Formalism: History–Doctrine*, 3rd ed. (New Haven: Yale University Press, 1981).

9 I have oriented the plans and diagrams that accompany this essay with north to the right (east down). This achieves the effect of heightening perception of the north-south intervals, since they are the ones that are therefore read from side to side (i.e., left to right and/or right to left), the privileged direction in reading. Moreover, this orientation is consistent with Le Corbusier's typical orientation of the Villa de Monzie/Stein site plan drawings as reproduced in *The Le Corbusier Archive*, ed. H. Allen Brooks, 32 vols. (New York: Garland Publishing Company & Paris: Fondation Le Corbusier, 1982–85), hereafter referred to as *LCA*, with drawings from the Fondation Le Corbusier hereafter referred to as FLC with relevant inventory numbers. See, for example, *LCA* vol. 3, *Le Corbusier: Palais de la Société des Nations, Villa Les Terrasses, and Other Buildings and Projects*, 1926–1927, FLC 10411, p. 370, and FLC 10565, p. 444 (here, Figures 16 and 17). Orientation of the plans and diagrams with north to the right establishes the site's longitudinal (north-south) axis as the horizontal or *x-axis* (abscissa) of the grid and the site's transverse (east-west) axis as the vertical or *y-axis* (ordinate) of the grid. Though it sounds paradoxical, keep in mind that the house's transverse axis corresponds to the site's longitudinal axis, and the house's longitudinal axis corresponds to the site's transverse axis.

10 Other commentators have addressed historical, morphological, and constructional aspects of Garches's grid. At least three studies have diligently traced the historical development of Le Corbusier's design of the grid. See Benton, *Villas of Le Corbusier*, pp. 164–189; Arjan Hebly, "The 5 Points and form," in Max Risselada, ed., *Raumplan and Plan Libre: Adolf Loos and Le Corbusier*, 1919–1930 (New York: Rizzoli International Publications, 1988; reprint ed., 1991), pp. 47–53; and Marc Dubois, "2 into 1," *Architectural Review*, January 1987, Volume CLXXXI, No. 1079, pp. 33–36. Barry Maitland's morphological analysis stands out as one of the unique attempts to examine the grid on a purely theoretical level; see Maitland, "The Grid," pp. 90–117. Attention has been devoted to the related mathematical problem of regulating lines, which, according to Le Corbusier, govern the principal facades. In particular, see Roger Herz-Fischler, "Le Corbusier's 'Regulating Lines' for the Villa at Garches (1927) and Other Early Works," *Journal of the Society of Architectural Historians*: volume 43, no. 1, March 1984, pp. 53–59. An attempt has also been made to relate the regulating lines to the plan in various diagrams. See Yucuru Tominaga and Shigetaka Nagao, "Rediscovery of Modern Housing/ Villa à Garches 1927," in *Space Design: A Monthly Journal of Art & Architecture* 133 (September 1975), pp. 66–71. Most relevant to the present study, perhaps, is Herz-Fischler's assertion, which is significant on many levels: "It is clear from the documents . . . that Le Corbusier did not hesitate to change his writings or drawings, after the fact, to accommodate his constantly changing views and systems. A consequence of this is that no serious study of Le Corbusier can be based on the "official" versions alone. *In particular, this is the case for Garches*," "Le Corbusier's 'Regulating Lines'," p. 57 (my emphasis). (See n. 60 below.) For a cogent discussion of the constructional aspects of the Dom-ino reinforced concrete frame system—the system employed at Villa de Monzie/Stein, of which the grid is an integral part and principal manifestation—see Eleanor Gregh, "The Dom-ino Idea," in *Oppositions* 15/16 (Winter/Spring 1979), pp. 60–87.

11 Rowe, *Mathematics of the Ideal Villa*, p. 8.

12 As published in "Mathematics of the Ideal Villa," p. 103, Rowe's 1947 diagram of the plan of Garches is oriented with north up. As published in *Mathematics of the Ideal Villa*, p. 5, fig. 1, Rowe's 1976 diagram of the plan is oriented with north to the right. Rowe informed me that this latter orientation was the result of an arbitrary layout decision made by the publisher; for reasons stated above (see n. 9), this is the way I have oriented recreations of both of his diagrams in this essay. The typographical error in Rowe's 1947 diagram, which mistakenly assigns the value 1 to the middle north-south bay, was corrected in the 1976 version.

13 The correlative issue that this difference raises, which involves the dialectic between *fact* and *implication*, is discussed in n. 30 below.

14 According to Herz-Fischler, Le Corbusier, in his article "Tracés régulateurs," *L'Architecture Vivante* (Spring–Summer 1929), pp. 12–24, "tells how the supporting frame gives a 2-1-2-1-2 cadence to the villa at Garches. This is referred to as an 'automatic system of proportioning' (*tracé que j'appelerai automatique*) and was used at Maison Cook, Pessac, and House C-2 at Stuttgart," "Le Corbusier's 'Regulating Lines'," p. 57.

15 Rudolf Wittkower, "Le Corbusier's Modulor," in Carlo Palazzolo and Riccardo Vio, eds., *In the Footsteps of Le Corbusier* (New York: Rizzoli International Publications, 1991), p. 13.

16 The extent to which Le Corbusier himself privileged the east-west, in contradistinction to his silence on the north-south, is reflected in this statement from the introduction to the section on Garches in his *Oeuvre complète* 1910–1929: *"La Maison est entièrement supportée par des poteaux disposés à équi-distance de 5 m et 2 m 5 sans souci du plan intérieur* (The house is supported entirely by columns that are placed at distances equal to 5 meters and 2.5 meters throughout the interior)" (my translation), p. 140. Le Corbusier neglects to clarify that this is true only with respect to the east-west spacing; therefore, he implies that the 5 and 2.5 meter intervals are used to determine the north-south placement of the columns as well, which, of course, is not the case.

17 Empirical evidence has helped to corroborate this. In the course of conducting my research, I have observed that both students and faculty colleagues can often recall accurately either the ABABA or 2:1:2:1:2 aspect of the grid, yet struggle in vain to recall correctly the intervals in the north-south direction.

18 When the subject of the grid of the villa at Garches has come up for discussion with students and colleagues at various schools of architecture over the years, no one has suggested the idea of *doubling* advanced here. Nor, according to my study of the published record, has this device been previously noted in print. I made the discovery in 1989 while teaching at the University of Texas at Arlington, where I conducted a graduate studio that involved an addition to the villa.

19 Rowe presumably delimits the projection of the terrace in his analytic diagrams in order to reinforce the comparison with the portico of the Villa Malcontenta, but he leaves the door open to confusion. The fact that the terrace actually extends an additional .5 (½) interval in the Le Corbusier-Rowe numbering system (this half interval also defines the zone of the stair that descends to the garden) appears to be an underappreciated point by many who have reprinted Rowe's diagrams. Among the authors whose discussions I have studied, only Kenneth Frampton aligns Rowe's diagram and Le Corbusier's plan in a manner that accurately and unambiguously indicates that the diagram does not include this additional important zone: first in "Frontality vs. Rotation," in *Five Architects: Eisenman, Graves, Gwathmey, Hejduk, Meier* (New York: Wittenborn & Company, 1972; reprint, New York: Oxford University Press, 1975), p. 11; and subsequently in *Modern Architecture: A Critical History*, p. 157. In another article, however, Frampton provides an example of the more common phenomenon, wherein the juxtaposition of diagram and plan is ambiguous and misleading; see "Le Corbusier and 'l'Esprit Nouveau'," *Oppositions* 15/16 (Winter/Spring 1979), p. 41.

20 My diagrams seek to represent the structural condition of the ground floor and *piano nobile* plans based on Le Corbusier's drawings reproduced in *LCA*, vol. 3. See, for example, ground floor plans FLC 10576, p. 452; FLC 10431, p. 382; and FLC 10451, p. 393. In the same volume, see *piano nobile* plans FLC 10563, p. 443; and FLC 10452, p. 393. The aforementioned plates are conclusive with respect to column locations; however they exhibit ambiguities with respect to column shapes, especially in the case of the inside two columns at the service entrance on the ground floor and their expressions at the *piano nobile*.

21 To my knowledge, only James Michael Ward, in his doctoral dissertation, "Le Corbusier's Villa 'Les Terrasses' and the International Style," New York University, 1984, has observed that the house has, as he writes, "thirty-one vertical supports," which agrees with my decipherment of Le Corbusier's ground floor plans reproduced in *LCA*, vol. 3 (see n. 20 above); see Ward, "Le Corbusier's Villa 'Les Terrasses'," pp. 178 and 207 n. 45. But Ward does not comment on the most stunning implication of this discovery, which is that Le Corbusier, by whatever mix of practical necessity and calculated artifice, violates the dictates of his idealized Dom-ino system and presents only the illusion of a cantilevered *piano nobile* at the north facade (the absence of columns at the *fenêtres en longueur* merely signifies that the floor above is cantilevered); at the south facade, however, by way of physical and conceptual opposition, the reality of the structural act of the cantilever at the *piano nobile* is unequivocally presented. It should be noted as well that Ward's research, ibid., pp. 19 and 53–56, uncovers the surprising fact that it was Gabrielle de Monzie, co-tenant with Sarah and Michael Stein, who held legal title to the land and assumed principal fiduciary responsibility for the construction of the villa. Villa de Monzie/Stein, therefore—as opposed to Villa Stein or even Villa Stein-de Monzie (though this is how the house is denominated in *LCA*), or the slightly different punctuational variation Villa Stein/de Monzie—perhaps more properly reflects the historical record. Le Corbusier evidently named the villa "Les Terrasses" (The Terraces), though he does not refer to it as such in the *Oeuvre complète* (it is simply called "Villa à Garches"). The drawings, other than the earliest few, which are stamped Stein de Monzie, bear the designation Mme G de Monzie (indicating, at the very least. that Le Corbusier clearly knew who was paying the bills).

22 Wittkower, "Le Corbusier's Modulor," p. 12; see Rowe, *Mathematics of the Ideal Villa*, p. 17 n. 6, where Rowe explicitly attributes his observations of the relationship between mathematics, musical harmony, and ideal proportion to his reading of Wittkower.

23 Rowe, *Mathematics of the Ideal Villa*, p. 8.

24 Rudolf Wittkower, *Idea and Image: Studies in the Italian Renaissance* (New York: Thames and Hudson, 1978), p.110.

25 Ibid., p. 110.

26 Ibid., p. 111.

27 Ibid., p. 111.

28 Ibid., p. 110.

29 Ibid., p. 110. Wittkower also ties the concept of musical consonance and arithmetical ratios to 15th- and 16th-century Italian aesthetics : "I do not suggest that Palladio or any other Renaissance artist translated musical into visual proportions; but they regarded the consonant intervals of the musical scale as the audible proofs for the beauty of the ratios of the small whole numbers," ibid., p. 112.

30 Peter Eisenman, in "Aspects of Modernism: Maison Dom-ino and the Self-Referential Sign," *Oppositions* 15/16 (Winter/Spring 1979), pp. 118–129, analyzes the general theoretical aspects of the issue of *extension* (tension) versus *stasis* (compression) implied by Le Corbusier's Dom-ino reinforced concrete frame system, of which the villa at Garches is a compound version. He observes, quite rightly, that the Dom-ino (Figure 8) implies, because of the location of the columns relative to the end of the floor slab, extension parallel to the long sides and stasis parallel to the short ends: "the location of the columns flush on the ends marks an opposition to the setback columns on the sides, and further suggests that the ends of the slab have been cut off, implying the possibility, or former condition, of horizontal extension of the slab on the long axis," ibid., p. 125. On one level, Eisenman's interpretation applies to the Dom-ino frame of Villa de Monzie/Stein. The coplanarity of columns and walls at the villa's ends, together with the horizontal banding of the north and south facades, which can be construed as finite plane-segments of planes that extend to infinity in either direction (i.e., east and west), confers upon the east-west intervals a centrifugal force; the implication is that this direction of the grid could resume/continue its ABA rhythm indefinitely. The north-south intervals, by contrast, because of the setback of the columns that form the cantilevers, can be construed as expressive of a self-contained, static system (i.e., a system that could not extend to include columns beyond the cantilevered slabs; this move would render the cantilevers meaningless); the implication is that, though the cantilevered slabs are themselves a dynamic structural expression and imply centrifugal projection, the column-slab system as a whole is at rest, static. That said, there is a counter-reading inherent to the Dom-ino, I believe. At Garches, the contingencies of the site and the particular plastic expression of the villa itself (including the *double-cantilever zone* that I describe later) underscore this reading and heighten the dialectic between fact and implication. Because of the shallow space of the site from side to side, the east-west intervals *cannot* extend—this direction of the grid may imply expansion, but the fact is that it stops—it is compressed, static. And because of the deep space of the site from front to back, there *is* physical extension of the north-south intervals—this direction of the grid may imply stasis, but the fact is that it does extend, it is dynamic. This counter-reading reinforces the idea that the north-south intervals— and not the east-west—constitute the dominant system at play in the physical expression and organizational structure of the villa and the site—a central (and new) idea that my analysis drives home in various ways. (For an elucidation of the 'deep space\shallow space' dialectic in Le Corbusier's work, see Thomas Schumacher, "Deep Space/Shallow Space," *Architectural Review*, January 1987, Volume CLXXXI, No. 1079, pp. 37–42.)

31 For articulation of the influential modernist concept of Significant Form, see Clive Bell, *Art* (Oxford: Oxford University Press, 1914; reprint, New York: Capricorn Books, 1958). See also my related article, "Significant Space," on-line at www.thearchitectpainter.com/MadisonGray/deep_SIGHT/SignificantSpace.htm.

32 Le Corbusier's enthusiasm for the reassuring authority of mathematics was tempered by his ultimate insistence on intuitive control of visual phenomena. On the one hand, he had confidence in what he called the "Q.E.D. of the mathematician"; see Herz-Fischler, "Le Corbusier's 'Regulating Lines'," p. 58. On the other hand, he extolled through musical metaphor (instruments) the ineffable faculty of artistic sense, acquired through painting: "The painter's [instrument] is his eye which truly acts as an instrument of control, verification, and penetration"; ibid., p. 58. Le Corbusier's faith in the connection between mathematics, painting (visual judgment), and music is interwoven in statements such as this (his emphasis): "*Architectural composition is geometric*, an event primarily of a visual nature; an event implying judgments of quantities, of relationships; the appreciation of proportions. Proportions provoke sensations; a series of sensations is like the melody in music," in Le Corbusier, *Precisions: on the Present State of Architecture and City Planning*, trans. Edith Schreiber Aujame (Cambridge, Massachusetts: The MIT Press, 1991), p. 133.

33 For Le Corbusier's veneration of the Parthenon, see in particular the chapter "Architecture, Pure Creation of the Mind" in Le Corbusier, *Towards a New Architecture*, trans. Frederick Etchells (London: Architectural Press, 1927; reprint, New York: Praeger Publishers, 1960), pp. 185–207. Le Corbusier, expressing his reverence in general for "creations of calculation," ibid., p. 212, as evidence of "the higher levels of the mind," ibid., p. 204, asserts that "the Parthenon gives us sure truths and emotion of a superior, mathematical order," ibid., p. 221.

34 Two examples of how Garches is typically understood in terms of the golden section, which can be deduced from study of the plates Le Corbusier published in the *Oeuvre complète*, are as follows: first, as indicated earlier (see n. 5 above), he includes the basic proportional assertion of the golden section on his drawing of the south facade, A:B=B:(A+B), to indicate that he has used this to organize its fundamental left-right (solid\void) proportional relationship. Thus, according to the east-west intervals along the bottom of his drawing, A=2+1=3, and B=2+1+2=5. Therefore, the ratio A:B=3:5. And the ratio B:(A+B)=5:8. The actual proportion of the golden section, which can be derived geometrically and arithmetically, is approximately .618 (a unique property of the golden section is that its reciprocal is the same number added to 1, i.e., 1.618). This is an irrational number that whole number ratios can only approximate; for example, the ratio of the numbers 3:5=.6, and the ratio of the numbers 5:8=.625. The ratio 5:8, which more nearly approximates the actual number, is the most common rationalized (that is, approximate) expression of the golden section, and one that Le Corbusier routinely used; second, this is seen in the second example of the regulating presence of the golden section, which relates the ratio of the sum of the north-south intervals to the sum of the east-west intervals of the enclosed part of the ground floor plan (that is, the ratio of the short side of the villa to the long side of the villa). In the Le Corbusier-Rowe system, the sum of the north-south intervals is ½+1½+1½+1½=5. The sum of the east-west intervals is 2+1+2+1+2=8. Thus their ratio is 5:8. This means that the enclosed rectangular field of the ground floor plan conforms to the conventional, idealized (whole number) ratio of the golden section. And, in theory, so does the rectangular vertical field of the north and south facades: the ratio of height to length is also 5:8. (In my doubled numbering system the ratio is correspondingly doubled and expressed as 10:16.) Rowe refers to this important approximation of the golden section—5:8—when describing the similarities between the volumetric proportions of Palladio's Villa Malcontenta and the Villa de Monzie/Stein at Garches: "both are blocks of corresponding volume, each measuring 8 units in length, by 5½ in breadth, by 5 in height," *Mathematics of the Ideal Villa*, p. 4; Rowe's point of reference for the breadth is the *piano nobile* plan (Garches's ground floor plan is 5 units in breadth). This is an example of the way in which Rowe's text has reinforced the association of the golden section—its whole number approximation—with the proportional structure of Garches. (See n. 60 below.)

35 For an explanation of Aristotle's concept of syntax or *taxis,* "the orderly arrangement of parts" of a formal system, which includes the double idea of the *grid* and *tripartition,* see Alexander Tzonis and Liane Lefaivre, *Classical Architecture: The Poetics of Order* (Cambridge, Massachusetts: The MIT Press, 1986), p. 9.

36 From an interview with Le Corbusier by Hugues Desalle, transcribed from an audio recording made six months before the architect's death and published in *Modulus/The University of Virginia School of Architecture Review* (1979), p. 71.

37 Perhaps the Derridean idea of the "double session"—"'displacement without reversal' of inherited concepts and categories"—provides the intellectual lens through which to view this alternative numerical and alphabetical reading of the Villa de Monzie/Stein's grid vis à vis Le Corbusier's own official view and popular terminology; see Christopher Norris, "Deconstruction, Post-modernism and the Visual Arts," in Christopher Norris and Andrew Benjamin, *What is Deconstruction?* (London: St. Martin's Press, 1988), p. 31. Also pertinent here, indeed fundamental to my argument throughout this book, is the concept of authorial or intentional fallacy, which is the "mistake" readers make in assuming that the author is the best critic of his/her own work, that is, that the author can reveal to us his/her intention. Instead, critics have come to realize that once a work of art is launched the author becomes to some degree simply one more reader and interpreter of the work.

38 Rowe, *The Mathematics of the Ideal Villa*, p. 4. Moreover, the significance of the cantilever to the visual and intellectual structure of the villa at Garches is central to Rowe's later essay, written with Robert Slutzky, "Transparency: Literal and Phenomenal," *Perspecta: The Yale Architectural Journal* 8 (1963), pp. 45–54. Max Risselada pursues the theme in "Free Plan versus Free Facade: Villa Savoye and Villa Baizeau revisited," Risselada, *Raumplan and Plan Libre*, pp. 55–63. He describes the confrontation of the free plan and free facade within Le Corbusier's projects: "This confrontation takes place in the zone created by the cantilever of the domino structural unit: the strip between the columns and the skin of the facade. It is this strip, which during the formulation of the 'five points', during the design process of Maison Cook and the villas Meyer and Stein-de Monzie respectively, was allotted an increasingly independent position," ibid., p. 56. According to Benton, Le Corbusier first introduced the cantilevered strip at the front facade only, *Villas of Le Corbusier*, pp. 174–75, which is ironic in light of the structural realities of the actual building (see n. 21 above).

39 Le Corbusier's preliminary drawings indicate that at one point in the design process the intervals were the same. Maitland identifies an early scheme "in which the building is five equal square bays wide" and principally two square bays deep, "The Grid," pp. 101–102. And Benton points out that Le Corbusier also experimented with ABA-based rhythms in both dimensions of the grid; *Villas of Le Corbusier*, p. 170. This condition is clearly expressed in Le Corbusier's site plan FLC 10411, *LCA*, vol.3, p. 370 (here, Figure 16).

40 Rowe, "Mathematics of the Ideal Villa," pp. 102 and 103; captions to the diagrams of the grids of the Villa Malcontenta and the villa at Garches.

41 "Standard framework of Le Corbusier's Domino House, designed in 1914, for mass-production, which shows how the quality of partial paralysis inherent in the plan of solid wall buildings such as Palladio's Villa Malcontenta is, in reinforced concrete structure, transferred to the section," Rowe, "The Mathematics of the Ideal Villa," p. 101.

42 In her summary of the architectural potential that may be attributed to the Dom-ino system, Gregh highlights the property of the module, explaining that "the reduction of the building to a few standardized elements provides the basis for systems of modular proportion," Gregh, "The Dom-ino Idea," p. 61. She notes, moreover, that this is "the first advantage noted by Jeanneret in his notes for the patent, in Sketchbook 1915–16, p. 58 (note 1)," ibid., p. 79 n. 2. Gregh suggests that the idea of the geometric module inherent in Le Corbusier's 1914 Dom-ino is ultimately the result of his dialectical mind, simultaneously empirical (practical) and Platonic (ideal): that is, the idea of the geometric module results from a conflation of the demands and benefits of industrial standardization (the economy and efficiency of standardized elements and measurements) on the one hand, and the metaphysical demands of pure mathematical proportions and rationalization on the other. According to Gregh, Le Corbusier wanted to create a constructional/architectural system "*based on the multiples and divisions of a geometric module*, like all great architecture of the past [my emphasis]" p. 68. On another level, Stanislaus von Moos refers to Joseph Paxton's Crystal Palace as the "birthplace of the 'module' in the architecture of the industrial age," in *Le Corbusier: Elements of a Synthesis* (Cambridge, Massachusetts: The MIT Press, 1980), p. 310. This observation descends from Wittkower, who asserts that Paxton's structure was the "first . . . of colossal size erected of standardized units over a grid. The logic inherent in the industrial revolution enforced a dimensional order," Rudolf Wittkower, "Le Corbusier's Modulor," in Carlo Palazzolo and Riccardo Vio, eds., *In the Footsteps of Le Corbusier* (New York: Rizzoli International Publications, 1991), p. 14.

43 For discussion of Le Corbusier's deployment of the 2.5-meter sliding window unit (composed of two 1.25-meter sashes), see Edward R. Ford, *The Details of Modern Architecture* (Cambridge, Massachusetts: The MIT Press, 1990), pp. 244–49.

44 Rowe writes that whereas Palladio preferred the triple division, it was "Le Corbusier's propensity to divide by four," Rowe, *Mathematics of the Ideal Villa*, p. 11. In the original text, Rowe gives the example that the facade is divided into four horizontal units (i.e., the four floors are clearly expressed at the south facade); "Mathematics of the Ideal Villa," p. 103. In addition to the various 1:4 relationships that regulate the window sub-divisions of the facades, which at the north effectively counter-subdivide the overall 20-meter length into 4 bays of 5 meters each (each bay is composed of 4 horizontal windows), four free-standing columns mark the threshold within the entrance hall, and the site is essentially divided into quadrants. The 1:4 ratio was a favorite of Le Corbusier's throughout his career. For example, he employed it at his mother's house in Vevey, 1923: there, the parallelepiped is 4 meters wide by 16 meters long.

45 Research by Benton and Hebly reveals the neo-classical preoccupation with center that underlies Le Corbusier's final ABABA rhythm of the east-west intervals. Hebly writes, for example: "Le Corbusier's approach suggests a width of 20 metres: 4 times a 5-metre bay. However, the centre is then occupied by a column, inconceivable in the front facade of the classic villa. This is the place for the entrance, certainly not for a column. Indeed, in all the early plans of this last version, the entrance is in the middle. . . . For the proportions of the house this means: one 5-metre bay in the middle, with a remainder of 7.5 metres at either side. These can only be divided into a half-bay of 2.5 metres and one of 5 metres," "The 5 Points and form," p. 52; see also Benton, *Villas of Le Corbusier*, p. 171.

46 The differentiation between facade and elevation is a result of my correspondence with Rowe. In response to an early draft of my article on Garches that preceded this book, Rowe wrote: "I think that your article would gain if, with reference to enclosing vertical planes, you were to introduce the designation *facade* as something distinct from *elevation* because though obviously related, after all these are, in the end, two very different species. So when does an elevation become a facade? And, in these matters, I tend to suppose that, almost always, a facade is a vertical surface endowed with some metaphorical or allegorical presence. Somewhat like the title page of say Palladio's *Quattro Libri*, it may be an announcement of content, but it may also conceal quite as much as it discloses. While in contradistinction, an elevation is a much more literal statement which, on occasion, may serve to convey certain important sectional information. But I also would attribute a privileged status to facade." This portion of the letter was published subsequently in *ANY: Architecture New York Magazine* 7/8 (1994), p. 5. Though Rowe employed this distinction to support the traditional view that the north and south (front and back) surfaces of Garches are facades, and the east and west (side) surfaces are elevations, I think the issue is more complex, the differentiation ultimately more equivocal. The west "elevation" (see Figure 9), for example, has attributes very much like the "facade" of Adolph Loos's Tzara House, which was constructed in Paris a year earlier (1925–26). I think it is likely that Le Corbusier saw Loos's project before he completed his design of Garches.

47 The site plan by Werner Seligmann is the basis for this observation (see n. 51 below). Seligmann confirmed in a conversation with me that his measurements of Garches show that the distance in front of the house to the boundary of the parking court is a square, completing a golden rectangle with the ground floor plan, as his published drawings imply; see Michael Dennis, *Court and Garden: From the French Hotel to the City of Modern Architecture,* (Cambridge, Massachusetts: The MIT Press, 1986), p. 200; and Frampton, "Le Corbusier and 'l'Esprit Nouveau'," p. 37. Dorothée Imbert's study, *The Modernist Garden* in France (New Haven: Yale University Press, 1993), also offers excellent commentary on the site of Villa de Monzie/Stein; however, it should be noted that her "'reconstituted site plan" (p. 155) is not in accord with Seligmann's on-site measurements with respect to the dimension (and proportional/mathematical implications) of the parking court. The site plan for one of Le Corbusier's early schemes, however, which Imbert reconstructs on the basis of FLC 10411, *LCA*, vol. 3, p. 370 (here, Figure 16), does agree with Seligmann; see Imbert, *Modernist Garden in France*, p. 157.

48 Le Corbusier, *Oeuvre complète* 1910–1929, p. 141.

49 The statement is specifically about his villa at Garches, in Le Corbusier, *Oeuvre complète* 1910–1929, p. 144. The translation is by von Moos, *Elements of a Synthesis*, p. 179.

50 Ibid., p. 179.

51 Seligmann graciously provided me with photocopies of his on-site measurements, which, though very difficult to decipher, helped me confirm the basis of his published partial site plans (see n. 47 above) and formulate my conjecture.

52 Review of the available documents, such as FLC 10565, *LCA*, vol.3, p. 444 (here, Figure 17), reveals Le Corbusier's basic intention to position the villa at the center of the site. But the documents are inconclusive with respect to the villa's micro-positioning as it relates to the *exact* center or slight shifts *off*-center that I conjecture here. Perhaps only through rigorous site reconnaissance, which requires on-site verification of the original property survey and new field-measurements, can this important issue be clarified.

53 According to Benton, the site is 26.9 meters wide, *Villas of Le Corbusier*, p. 166. According to Hebly, it is 27 meters wide, "The 5 Points and form," p. 51. According to FLC 10447, *LCA*, vol. 3, p. 391, the site is 26.9 meters wide. The *idealized* site plan that I conjecture would require a site-width of 27.5 meters: the east property line setback is slightly less than the idealization requires in order to obtain a full interval of 4 (5 meters).

54 See, for example, my article "Collage Reading: Braque|Picasso." *Proceedings: 84th ACSA Annual Meeting & Technology Conference* (Washington: ACSA Press, 1996), pp. 181–187.

55 Inspired by Rem Koolhaas and Bruce Mau, *S,M,L,XL* (New York: Monacelli Press, 1995).

56 Le Corbusier, *Towards a New Architecture*, p. 191.

57 For an elucidation of the idea of the "split-screen" in Le Corbusier's work, see Thomas Schumacher, "Deep Space/Shallow Space," *Architectural Review*, January 1987, Volume CLXXXI, No. 1079, pp. 37–42.

58 Le Corbusier's description of the Villa de Monzie/Stein is quoted by Herz-Fischler, "Le Corbusier's Regulating Lines," p. 59. The translation is slightly different in Le Corbusier, *Precisions*, p. 72.

59 Wittkower, *Idea and Image*, p. 122.

60 In the continuation of a passage noted previously (see n. 10 above), Herz-Fischler maintains that "no serious study of Le Corbusier can be based on the 'official' versions alone. In particular, this is the case for Garches; as *the various early documents and drawings indicate, Le Corbusier made no use of the golden number in its design* [my emphasis]," Herz-Fischler, "Le Corbusier's Regulating Lines," p. 57. According to Herz-Fischler, Le Corbusier's regulating lines, which are an expression of the incommensurable golden number proportional system, were applied to the facade drawings that appear in the *Oeuvre complète* after the project was completed. On the other hand, von Moos points to "Matila Ghyka, *Esthétique des proportions dans la nature et dans les arts* (Paris, 1927), where Ghyka publishes and discusses some of Le Corbusier's proportion studies, especially the regulating lines of the Villa Stein at Garches," von Moos, *Elements of a Synthesis*, p. 366 n. 98. Thus the very year the villa was completed, Ghyka used it to show how Le Corbusier had employed golden number regulating lines. However, von Moos also seems to lend indirect support to Herz-Fischler's theory of post-facto regulating lines: "There can be no doubt that Ghyka's book [*Le Nombre d'Or*, published in Paris in 1931] played an important role in Le Corbusier's coming to grips with the problem of the golden section in nature and art," ibid., p. 310. One might well conclude that while regulating lines were not part of Le Corbusier's design process at Villa de Monzie/Stein, use of the geometrical approximation of the golden section surely was. Le Corbusier's interest in the golden number, both in architecture and painting, predates the villa at Garches. And the iconic whole-number approximation of the golden ratio—8:5—is an undeniable property of the villa's basic physical relationships, which surely cannot be explained as a post-facto phenomenon (see n. 34). Interestingly enough, of the four original illustrations of Rowe's 1947 text, the one of Matila Ghyka's harmonic decompositions of the golden rectangle is the only one that is not included in the 1976 edition; see Rowe, "Mathematics of the Ideal Villa, " p. 104. See Herz-Fischler, "Le Corbusier's Regulating Lines," p. 58 n. 9, for insight and commentary on Rowe's omission of this illustration in the 1976 edition and on the issue of the direct influence of Ghyka's book on Le Corbusier's mathematical ideas.

61 Wittkower, *Idea and Image*, p. 116.

62 Herz-Fischler, "Le Corbusier's Regulating Lines," p. 59.

63 Ibid., p. 59; except where noted, italicized passages are Le Corbusier's emphasis.

64 Ibid., p. 57.

65 The idealized height of the villa expressed in whole-number y (1-meter) modules is equal to 12 (12 meters), which equals 9.6 x (1.25-meter) modules. The idealized height of the villa expressed in whole-number x (1.25-meter) modules is equal to 10 (12.5 meters), which equals 12.5 y (1-meter) modules—10 derives from the whole-number approximation of the golden section ratio, 16:10 (see n. 34 below). Both 12 meters and 12.5 meters represent satisfactory approximations of the golden section ratio in relation to the width of the villa, which equals 20 meters (12.5 is slightly more accurate). The documents are inconclusive as to the definitive height of the villa, and given that Le Corbusier's modus operandi was to continually make trade-offs between idealizations and empirical demands, one should not be surprised to learn that the villa as detailed in the construction documents or as built may not be in precise accord with either of these two dimensions. Ultimately, this conflict between idealism and pragmatism infuses the project on every level.

Le Corbusier, Villa de Monzie/Stein, Garches, 1927. Le Corbusier's friends, including Piet Mondrian (hand on ladder, lower right), pose for group shot on roof. © FLC L1(10)75.

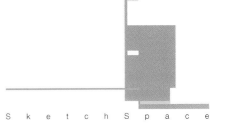

S k e t c h S p a c e

SketchSpace

My architectural aesthetic springs from the abstract systems I explore in my paintings. 1

But I believe that a great building also fuses Story and Form 2

— and stirs the observer's emotions. 3

An advanced architecture provides not only shelter, 4

presents not only a refined system of organizational and optical devices applied to materials. 5

An advanced architecture also tells stories, constructs metaphors through art, 6

and thereby creates an *extraordinary world*—not only for the eyes, but also for the soul. 7

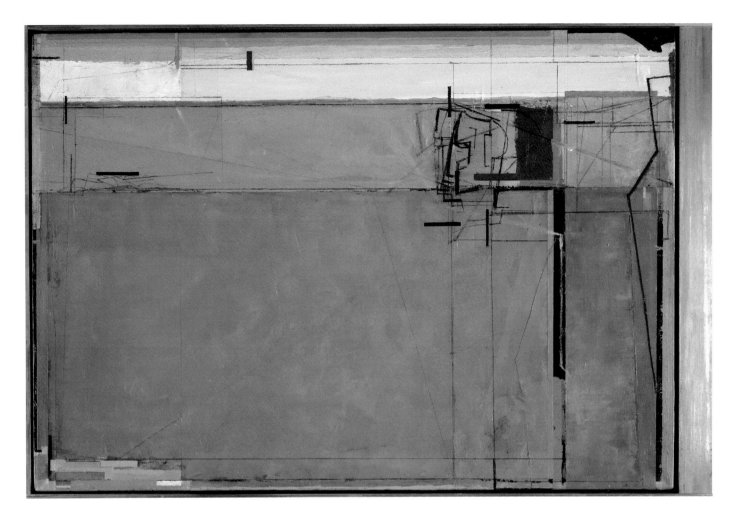

GARCHES STUDY _3 / **DAEDALUS** (AKA *AENEAS* : *SELF-PORTRAIT* : *THE KNIGHT*). 1996.
Oil on canvas in aluminum frame + pencil (grease, charcoal, graphite). 24.625 x 38.5 in. | Private Collection, Boston, MA

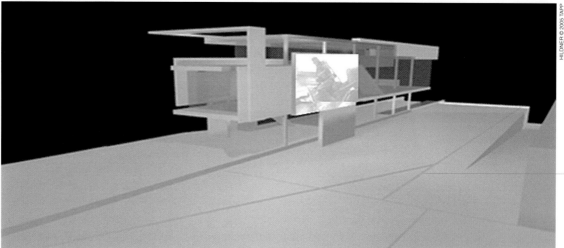

LONGITUDINAL PROJECTION HOUSE — **AKA CINEMA HOUSE | DIEBENKORN CHESS HOUSE**. JEF7REY HILDNER ARCHITECT | CINEMATECT® 2001

Assistants: Philip Speranza, Jonathan Cicconi, Augusto Castro, Orlando Pissaro

www.thearchitectpainter.com/surface_7ARCHITECT/diebenkornCHESS_house.htm

LONGITUDINAL PROJECTION HOUSE — AKA CINEMA HOUSE | DIEBENKORN CHESS HOUSE

HILDNER © 2005 TAPP

HILDNER © 2005 TAPP

JIGSAW KNIGHT | SIGNIFICANT SPACE — **AKA DAEDALUS HQ**. JEF7REY HILDNER. Acrylic and charcoal on canvas. 24 x 36 in. | 1997
www.thearchitectpainter.com/surface_7ARCHITECT/paintings/displacementCutFigures_1997.htm

ARCHITECTURE IS A STORY TOLD THROUGH BUILDING.

ARCHITECT, PAINTER, AND WRITER JEF7REY HILDNER launched The Architect Painter Press in 2005 under the banner, "Live Brave." The Architect Painter Press presents Hildner's buildings, paintings, and insights—work that reflects his focus on the visible and invisible architecture of life and art. The Architect Painter Press also seeks to present the work of other artists. Current titles range from Hildner's books Visual Ef9ects, Daedalus 9, Henry Trucks — Painter, Picasso Lessons, and Garches 1234 to his books Metaphysical Warrior and Live Brave. His work also appears in a wide array of other venues—for example, Architectural Record, Journal of Architectural Education, ANY, Oz, The Christian Science Monitor, IMDb, and Global Architecture Houses. The book Architectural Formalism, by Hakan Anay, features Hildner's essay "Formalism: Move | Meaning" alongside essays by theorists Rosalind Krauss, Peggy Deamer, Robert Slutzky, and Colin Rowe. Hildner received an Association of Collegiate Schools of Architecture award for excellence in teaching. His project Dante | Telescope House won the New Jersey Chapter of The American Institute of Architects "Blue Ribbon Award for Excellence in Design." He paints under the name Henry Trucks. He writes under the names Madison Gray, Eliot Plum, and Michelangelo A. Roland Slate. Hildner's one-word life theme—architecture—shapes his quest, his outlook, and his output, including his work as screenwriter and story architect. He earned his undergraduate and graduate degrees from Princeton University.

ARCHITECTURE IS THE STAGE

(D)ANTE | TELESCOPE HOUSE / 1991–1996. PHOTOGRAPH © YUKIO FUTAGAWA | GA PHOTOGRAPHERS. GA HOUSES 51, 1997

A shard of ancient suns — the steel-beam Telescope of the Dante | Telescope Monolith sights the North Star.
Iconic proportions shape the wall-as-canvas Dante | Telescope Monolith (depth : width : height) **1 : 4 : 9** —
the cube of the first three integers: **1   2   3**

SET FOR THE DRAMA OF LIFE.
ARCHITECTURE IS THE WORLD MADE VISIBLE THROUGH FORM.

THE SPANISH CONN

Spain stands for artistic freedom. For radical, forward-thinking aesthetic expression. For uncons
inquiry. In the spirit of her people who navigated and explored the globe, Spain stands for bold adventure
For the progressive and avant-garde in LITERATURE, PAINTING, ARCHI

So does New York City. So does Columbia University.

cervantes picasso g

1605 | Don Quixote
Inventor of the Novel

1907 | Les Demoiselles d'Avignon
Inventor of Cubism Fountainhead of Modern Art

1905-1
Invent
iconoclastic li

The Casa Hispanica 2007|2008 springs to life in restless strange form true to its

All art tends towar

1605/1615   1907   1905-1910   1908   2008

Architecture is the assertion, unreflective or conscious, of an aesthetic system and the plastic and philosophical/ontological values that sus
architectures the plastic system (visible form) and the intellectual premises (invisible meaning) are highly refined and lucid. and their inter
inextricable, resonates with the unmistakable authority of *Significant*
The work of CINEMATECT STUDIOS & FORMFINDING STUDIOS involves more than the surface aesthetics of materials and light. It involves
architecture's visual and metaphysical structure . . . toward the making of significant buildings of unexpected magnitudes for human inhab

LA NUEVA CASA HISPANICA

JEF7REY HILDNER ARCHITECT
C I N E M A T E C T™
S T U D I O S

ECO   UNANUMO   ORTEGA Y GASSET   JUAN GRIS

CERVANTES

CTION

d intellectual
overy, and risk.

udi

a Mila, Barcelona
trange Buildings
f plastic genius and expressive power

ry and soul

uring the contradiction between that which appears and that which signifies, between

FORM MASTERS
STORY TELLERS

FORM   MEANING
Borges   Robert Slutzky

LITERATURAS HISPANICAS

n advanced
ship, ultimately

Form & Content

-surface of

e Borges

9

LITERATURAS HISPANICAS

2007 COLUMBIA UNIVERSITY

ARCHITECTURE IS THE WORLD BETWEEN

WALLS.

ARCHITECTURE IS THE WORLD IN A BUILDING

CERVANTES

LA NUEVA CASA HISPÁNICA. COLUMBIA UNIVERSITY. 2007 | PENTHOUSE: CERVANTES ROOM. RICHARD ATCHISON ARCHITECT & JEF?REY HILDNER ARCHITECT

FILM IS THE M
CINEMATEC

"Now and forever the architect is going to replace the set designer. The movies will be the faithful

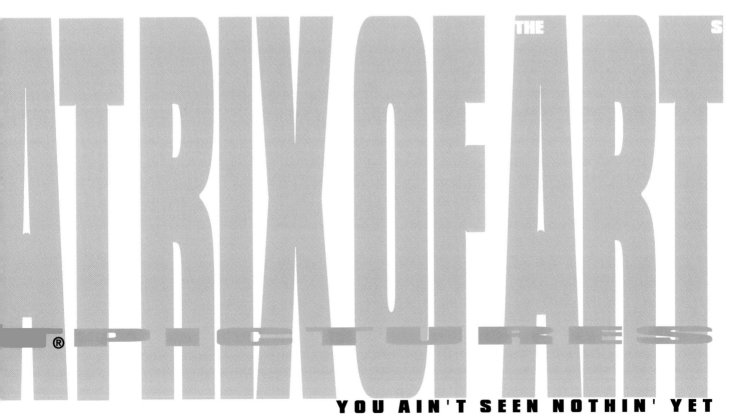

THE
ATRIX OF ART
® PICTURES

YOU AIN'T SEEN NOTHIN' YET
translator of the architect's boldest dreams." — Luis Buñuel | 1927 (After seeing Fritz Lang's *Metropolis*)

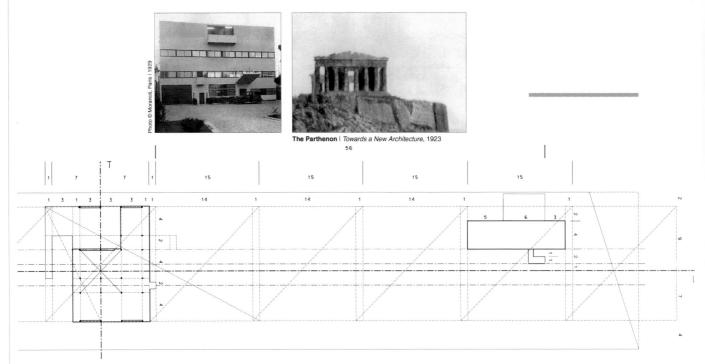

Photo © Morancé, Paris | 1929

The Parthenon | *Towards a New Architecture*, 1923

56

When I undertook the writing of this book, I accepted it as my duty to review the whole question in detail and in chronological order, so that the salient points might emerge, the principle become clear, that everything might become simple and natural, accessible to the minds of others and therefore also . . . vulnerable, open to attack as to useful pursuit.

— Le Corbusier

ABSTRACT. It is now fifty years since Colin Rowe's celebrated essay first revealed what Le Corbusier had concealed about the mathematics of the neo-Palladian structural grid of Villa de Monzie/Stein at Garches (1927)—namely, the ratios of the structural intervals that define the organization of the villa from front to back. The importance of this discovery, reported in Rowe's "The Mathematics of the Ideal Villa: Palladio and Le Corbusier compared" (1947), has been underappreciated in subsequent scholarship, which has focused instead on Rowe's discovery of the accord between Garches and Palladio's Villa Malcontenta (c. 1550–1560) with respect to the so-called ABABA rhythm of the intervals from side to side. However, the north-south intervals are no less essential to a proper apprehension of Le Corbusier's structural/ spatial grid as a complete idea. This article reexamines the mathematics of the grid employed at Villa de Monzie/Stein and proposes an alternative to the Le Corbusier-Rowe numbering system. The alternative system heightens perception of the grid's fundamental mathematical elegance and ideality as well as its comprehensive control of the "extended field" of the site and elevations/facades. This study seeks to cast new light on the significance of Le Corbusier's assertion that, at Garches, more than at any of his other projects, "proportion ruled absolutely there, as absolute mistress."

"Remembering the Mathematics of the Ideal Villa"
by Jef7rey Hildner
Journal of Architectural Education, 52 (1999): pp 143–162.

www.jstor.org/stable/1425460
+
www.onlinelibrary.wiley.com/doi/10.1111/j.1531-314X.1999.tb00265.x/abstract

For all links to the archive of the original referred essay on which this book is based, go to:

www.archive.org/details/GARCHES1234

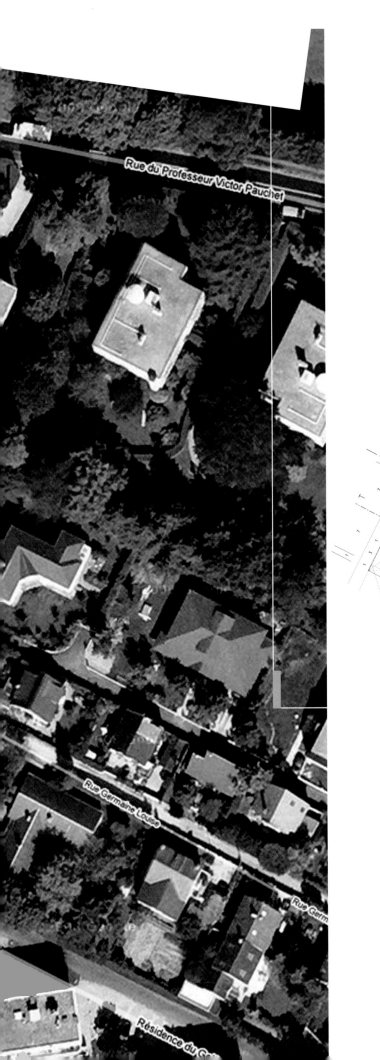

GREEN STRIPE

Aerial view of Villa Garches 2009. Shows orientation relative to true north. (Google Maps)

Note the positive\negative chess game of S, M, L, XL geometric cut-figures within the rectangular field—on the green-stripe chess-board—of the outdoor room.

Le Corbusier struck a balance between architecture as solid and void: space-occupier and space-definer.

And through his hard-won mastery, all elements click.

REMEMBERING THE MATHEMATICS OF THE IDEAL VILLA: AN ESSAY ON LE CORBUSIER'S 1927 VILLA DE MONZIE/STEIN

GARCHES 1234

JEFFREY HILDNER

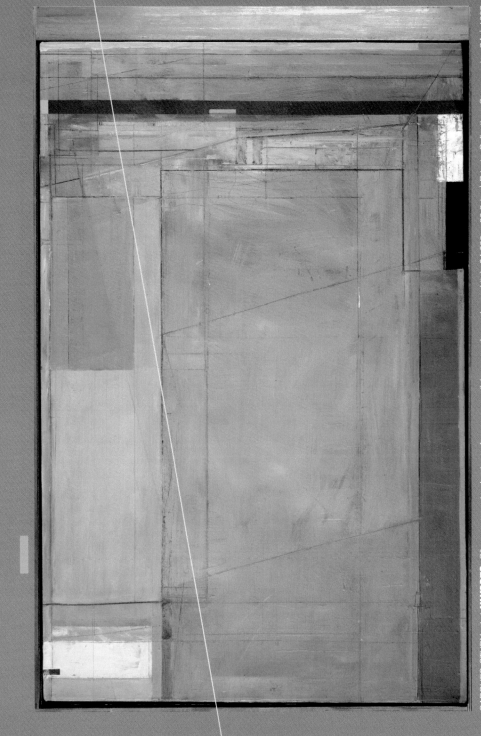

GARCHES STUDY _1 / **ULYSSES**. Oil on canvas in aluminum frame + pencil (grease, charcoal, graphite). 24.625 x 38.5 in. | Private Collection, Sacramento, CA | 1997

IN 1927, THE GREAT SWISS-FRENCH ARCHITECT LE CORBUSIER completed a house in the Paris suburb of **Garches**.

The house has become an icon of modern architecture.

Other major architectural events took place that year: Konstantin Melnikov built his cylinder house in Moscow; Alvar Aalto won the competition for the design of the Viipuri Library in Vyborg, Russia; Pierre Chareau began work on the Maison de Verre in Paris; and sixteen leading architects of the modern movement, including Le Corbusier, showcased projects for working-class housing at the Weissenhof exhibition in Stuttgart. And in the new medium of cinema, 1927 featured Fritz Lang's landmark film *Metropolis*—stunning audiences with visions of how buildings in the future could look.

But no structure of the early modernist era has gained more renown than Le Corbusier's **VILLA DE MONZIE/STEIN** at Garches. In 1947, British scholar **COLIN ROWE'S** essay "The Mathematics of the Ideal Villa" brought Garches to the foreground. And Garches—as architects refer to the house—has stayed there ever since.

ARCHITECT JEF7REY HILDNER revisits the mathematics of the ideal villa. He uncovers Rowe's oversights and sweeps away the mythologies about Garches that Rowe's essay generated. In addition, Hildner's analysis and drawings reveal new aspects of Le Corbusier's work that have remained hidden until now.

GARCHES 1234 picks up where Rowe's essay left off and throws bold light on Le Corbusier's assertion that at Garches, more than any of his other projects, "proportion ruled absolutely there, as absolute mistress."

HILDNER published an early version of this essay in the refereed *Journal of Architectural Education*. Here the essay appears in its final and fully illustrated

FORM.

VISUAL EF9ECTS
ARCHITECTURE AND THE CHESS GAME
OF FORM & STORY

"Architecture is a silver coin.

Inscribed on one side, *FORM:*
Architecture is the stage set for the drama of life.

Inscribed on the other side, *STORY:*
Architecture is a story told through a building."

—JEF7REY HILDNER

ARCHITECTURE IS A CHESS GAME OF FORM & STORY WAGED ON THE BATTLEFIELD OF A BUILDING AND ITS SITE

IN **VISUAL EF9ECTS**
THE ARCHITECT PAINTER JEF7REY HILDNER
builds on signature themes and concepts he
lays out in *Daedalus 9*. The basis of his talk
for the Symposium on Formalism (2016) at
the Syracuse University School of Architecture
Program in Florence, *VISUAL EF9ECTS* reflects
Hildner's quest to design buildings that trade in
the Silver Coin of Architecture: an architecture
that presents a creative demonstration of the
Chess Game of Art, where the White Knight
of Form (Aesthetics) and the Black Knight
of Story (Symbolics) team up to make a
SIGNIFICANT ARCHITECTURE.

SILVERKNIGHTARCHITECTURE
KnightHeadQuarters

The White Army of FORM cries,
"ARCHITECTURE IS THE STAGE SET FOR THE DRAMA OF LIFE."

The Black Army of STORY cries,
"ARCHITECTURE IS A STORY TOLD THROUGH A BUILDING."

**IN VISUAL EF9ECTS,
ARCHITECT JEF7REY HILDNER**
BUILDS ON SIGNATURE THEMES AND
CONCEPTS THAT HE LAID OUT IN HIS
BOOK DAEDALUS 9, TURNING AGAIN
TO THE CINEMATIC METAPHOR OF
CHESS TO BRING HIS THEORY OF
ARCHITECTURE TO LIFE. AN AWARD-
WINNING SCREENWRITER AS WELL
AS AN AWARD-WINNING ARCHITECT,
HILDNER TRANSPOSES INSIGHTS FROM
THE ARENA OF STORY ARCHITECTURE
TO HIS PARALLEL ARENA OF BUILDING
ARCHITECTURE. VISUAL EF9ECTS
REFLECTS HIS QUEST TO DESIGN
BUILDINGS THAT PRESENT A CREATIVE
DEMONSTRATION OF THE CHESS GAME
OF ART, WHERE THE WHITE ARMY OF
FORM (AESTHETICS) AND THE BLACK
ARMY OF STORY (SYMBOLICS) BATTLE
FOR OUR MIND AND SOUL AND HEART—
FORM & STORY FIGHT TO CREATE A
HEART-POUNDING WORK OF ART.

THE SILVER KNIGHT OF FORM & STORY

MY AVATAR

7

LIFE-SIZE CHESS GAME ON PALACE SQUARE, ST. PETERSBURG, 1924

THE ARCHITECT PAINTER

THE ARMIES OF FORM & STORY FIGHT THE WAR OF ART.
THEY FIGHT FOR OUR MIND AND SOUL AND HEART.

BOOKS BY JEF7REY HILDNER (aka ELIOT PLUM and HENRY TRUCKS) **:**

FORM & STORY